Plants
&Flowers
in the Home

Plants & Flowers
in the Home

Violet Stevenson

TREASURE PRESS

Contents

First published in Great Britain
by Sundial Books Ltd

This edition published by
Treasure Press
59 Grosvenor Street
London W1

© 1975 Hennerwood
Publications Ltd

Reprinted 1983, 1984

ISBN 0 907407 88 9

Printed in Hong Kong

Introduction

Decoration with growing plants has always been popular and although we sometimes read of 'contemporary' plants, the pot plant in the home is no recent introduction. It is the way that plants are used that has changed so tremendously during the past two decades. A plant is no longer an afterthought. It is an embellishment, an applied decoration, lasting longer than fresh cut flowers and in so many senses, serving a fuller purpose. Plants are a necessity. They add to our happiness and our tranquillity. They are living things and so easy to live with.

Where at one time plants seemed to stand isolated in a home, usually on a sill or in a window, having no real share in the homely things around them, they now play an important decorative role. In this book we shall see how plants can be used both with and in lieu of furnishings. We shall see how to draw them into the general theme of home decoration. How to place them, how to use them to advantage in more ways than one, how to mix them and arrange them and, of course, how to buy, grow and care for them.

Most people begin by buying their plants. Some continue to do so but there are others who discover that they would like to raise some plants of their own. This subject will also be discussed – fortunately, so many house plants can be raised easily from cuttings.

Not all house plants bloom and not all of those which do have conspicuous or even beautiful flowers, at least not when seen with the naked eye. However most people want flowers as well as leaves around them. So after describing the house plants we can grow well, we shall go on to discuss how fresh flowers can be arranged and used to the greatest advantage. And from the display of fresh flowers, whose lives alas are so fleeting, it is a short, logical step to arranging dried flowers.

These, like today's plants, also play a new role. With plants, dried flowers share the estimable quality of remaining lovely for long periods in warm interiors – in rooms which often are responsible for cut flowers maturing and so fading, too quickly. Central heating calls for its own kind of decoration!

Dried flowers can look as attractive as any other kind. Gone is the Victorian dust-trapping birds' nest type of bouquet of immortelles and grasses and in its place we can have both modern and classically styled flower arrangements, montage and all kinds of decorative designs, if these are required. In these, the old favourite flowers are combined with a wealth of new 'perpetuelles' now drawn from all parts of the globe and on sale everywhere. Dried flowers are delightful complements to green, living plants and they can stand between a plant and some source of dry heat, an attractive but effective barrier, protecting the plant in a convenient manner since so many plants need a humid atmosphere.

Once you have arranged flowers many times it will become natural to think also of arranging plants. These can be treated in much the same way as flowers and grouped together still in their pots in temporary arrangements or else given a more permanent value and beauty by transplanting them and mixing them in a larger container.

Once you have seen how attractive such arrangements can be you will not hesitate to take that short step to making pot-et-fleur, mixing plants and cut flowers. Indeed you might begin unprompted simply by enlivening a bowl of plants which look past their best. You will soon appreciate that this is another fascinating form of flower arrangement in its widest sense.

Throughout this book are examples of many ways in which all these subjects have been and can be used. While it is hoped that the reader will find them attractive and appealing enough to want to copy them, it is also hoped that this book will become an inspiration to all who love plants and who would like to arrange them instead in his or her own special individual way. Through it we hope to promote a much wider use of plants and flowers in the home.

House Plants

Understanding plants

If our plants are to remain decorative for as long as possible we have to get to know and understand them. First of all we should realise that a house plant is not really any different from a garden or wild plant except in as much as we have brought it into the home. It is special because it is attractive and adaptable. A house plant is one that is grown indoors under normal living conditions.

Yet often our living conditions are not those of the plant if it were growing naturally. House plants have become such because of their adaptability—we really should call them home plants. How marvellous it is that a plant which comes from the dim, steamy jungle, can live cosily inside four walls in different climate and soil and that next to it a cactus from the hot, arid desert will bloom on a sunny kitchen windowsill.

Indoor plants vary just as much as those which grow out of doors for there are herbaceous kinds, shrubs, trees, climbers and creepers, bulbs, tubers, corms and rhizomes. There are perennials, biennials and annuals. There are evergreen and deciduous plants. There are those we prize for their foliage and others which we admire for their flowers. There are even some indoor plants we grow for their fruits. There are plants to suit us all and the different ways in which we live.

For the sake of convenience house plants are divided into two groups, temporary and permanent plants. The terms speak for themselves although one should realise that permanent needs to be taken at its hairdresser's value. Generally speaking, the temporary plants may be considered to have a life, once brought into the home, which is measured in weeks while that of the permanent plants may be measured in months or even years. We should aim for years. Fortunately many are both agreeable and adaptable.

The temporary plants are more familiar to more people than the permanent kinds. They include such flowering kinds as azaleas, cyclamen, heaths, primulas, cinerarias, the berried solanums and capsicums and the ornamental leaved coleus, the scented exacum and bromeliads. All of which have been grown with one aim; that they should be at their best when they reach the customer. It is only natural that one should want the flowers to go on as long as possible. Yet what so often happens is that from the moment the plant is brought into the home its flowers slowly but steadily decline in beauty and life. This need not happen. If we can learn

Previous page
Solanum capsicastrum. Unless it is in cool surroundings this little plant cannot be expected to live for long in the home. Water it carefully, spray the entire plant with clean tepid water daily and keep it as far as possible from any source of heat.

Left
Bromeliads. Two species of the bromeliad cryptanthus. The tallest is *C. bromelioides* 'Tricolor' of which the young growth is often rose-tinted, the other, *C. fosterianus* is distinguished by its across-the-leaf markings. These are excellent plants as they thrive in most normal home conditions.

Below
Aechmea fasciata. This is one of the easiest of all house plants to grow, and to water; simply keep the centre vase always full. The inflorescence is both brilliantly coloured and long-lasting. It may be increased by offsets such as can be seen low left.

Right
Many new species of cacti are constantly being introduced, and those already familiar to cacti-lovers have become great favourites. *Parodia microsperma* shown here comes from Argentina, and is a member of a large family of cacti many of which are easy to cultivate.

Below
Cryptanthus zonatus. This is an agreeable cryptanthus (known as the Zebra plant) which lends itself to all kinds of decorative schemes. It can be grown in a pot, in mixed arrangements, used in pot-et-fleur or even fixed with other small bromeliads to a mossed branch. The leaves can grow up to 9 inches in length.

to appreciate the plant's needs we ought to be able to enjoy it to the full. Fortunately, it does not take long to get to know plants.

The four things that plants get in their early days that help them to grow and give them a good start in life are: warmth, light and humidity, steady temperature and freedom from draughts. Of these basic requirements of a healthy plant, we are normally able to supply only warmth and light. For in our homes temperatures tend to fluctuate, usually they rise to a peak in the evening and then swiftly drop during the night. We may pride ourselves on the air in our rooms being nice and dry, yet our plants need humidity. It is really surprising what plants will put up with. It is also surprising how easy it is to give them what they need. It so happens, as we shall see, that in making a plant comfortable, in ensuring that it shall live as long as possible, we also make it more decorative. It settles in more attractively. It becomes part of the environment.

As you would expect, those plants which are most popular, most often seen, are the toughest. The same goes for those which have been around for a long time such as aspidistras, palms of many kinds, rubber plants and ivies. If you see the same kind of plant growing well under many different conditions it follows that this is an easy type and if you are new to house plants you would do well to get one like it.

Indoor plants are rather like pets. They have different habits, different needs, according to their kind. You will get to know a plant as you would get to know a pet. For instance, one kind of plant may need watering just

The sansevieria, tough and
adaptable, will live for years. It
is highly decorative and
provides splendid contrasts of
colour, texture and shape to
groups and arrangements,
demonstrated here in a group
which includes a scindapsus,
Pelargonium crispum and
peperomias.

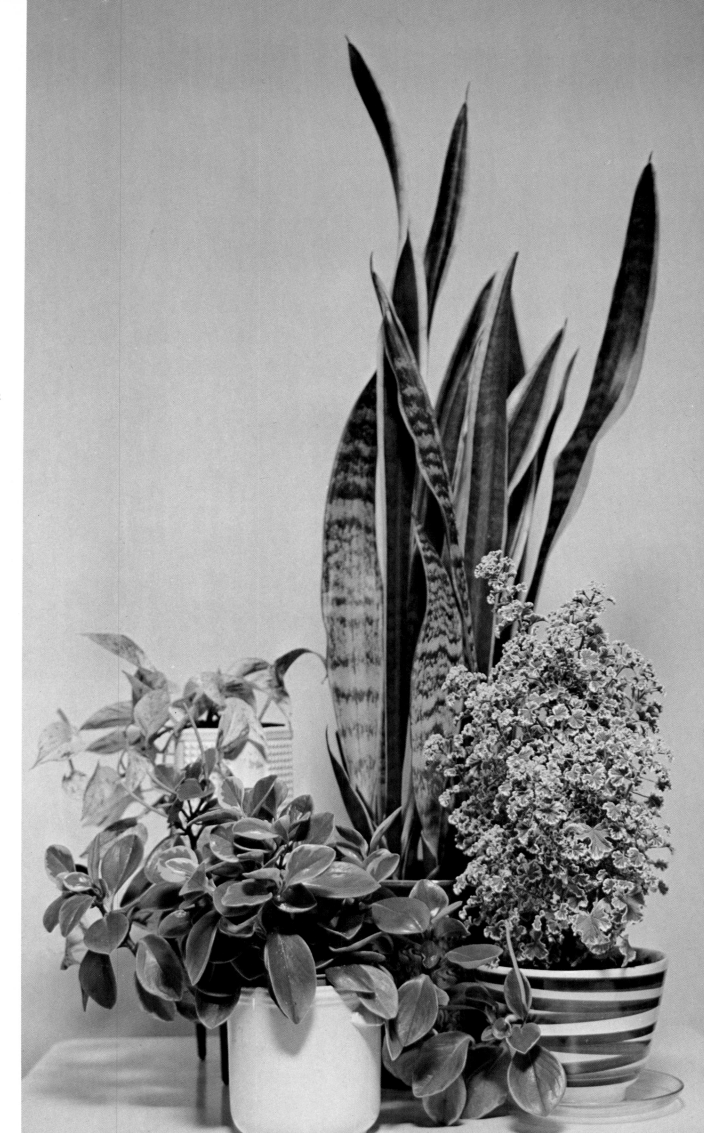

once a week, but should it stand in a very sunny, well ventilated yet warm room, it may sometimes need watering every day. It is important for the new indoor gardener to realize that he or she is very much in command. Mostly, someone who cannot see either the plant or its setting can do no more than generalize.

Fortunately, there are a few plants which are so tough, so house or home-hardy, that it is possible to give fairly precise directions for certain aspects of their care. These ensure that the plants live. Whether they thrive, flourish and even flower is in the hands of the plant owner.

Among these easy-going types are some in a family known as bromeliads. The pineapple is a typical, though tall, member and because a bromeliad other plants belonging to this family are known as room pines. While it is possible to grow an ordinary pine-apple indoors and even to have it bear fruit, it is the lovely variegated forms which are most often seen.

Possibly the best known of the family is *Aechmea fasciata* the Greek vase or urn plant. The vernacular name comes from the shape of the plant, the bases of its leaves overlap and form a vase in which water will remain. This reservoir is a characteristic of bromeliads. Some have a more pronounced vessel than others but it is effective all the same. In the wild state and growing on trees, the plants trap their water this way. In the home, where they are mostly grown in pots of soil they can still take their water this way though it is also possible to grow them on wood. It is comforting to know that all you have to do is to keep the centres filled with water.

There are several species and varieties of bromeliads on sale and it is possible gradually to make a collection. Cryptanthus species are flatter and more star-like than the tall aechmeas. Vriesia and neoregelia come between the two. All have strange, handsome markings and some are vividly coloured with brilliant reds and coral pinks. They produce odd, and tiny or conspicuous and strangely beautiful flowers. They look so wonderfully exotic that it is hard to believe that they really are easy – but they are. They live for years and after flower-ing they send up new shoots or offsets from which you can propagate more plants. They will grow in many places in a home, from a fireplace to a sunny window. Some of them are delightful subjects in mixed arrange-ments of plants or plants and flowers which are known as pot-et-fleur.

Resembling the taller bromeliads in some ways with its long pointed leaves and handsome leaf markings, the sansevieria, a member of the lily family, shares their agreeable toughness and adaptability. It too will live for years and will grow so large in time, widthways not in height, that you can either divide it into several smaller plants or repot it into containers of ever-increasing girth and so allow both it and your reputa-tion as an indoor gardener to grow to a great size.

Its right to be included in the easy plant group is due to the fact that you can water it in the same way as you water cacti, once a month from October to March and then once a week. During summer a little soluble plant food will be welcome.

The sansevierias have thick chunky leaves. They are semi- or sub-succulent and as such are able to store water. This is the reason why they can be left unwatered for so long. Too much water poured into the pot soil will cause the leaves to rot at their bases.

They also are plants which will grow almost any-where, even tolerating low temperatures from time to time. They tend to remain static where conditions are not really to their liking and often you will find that if a plant is moved to some more agreeable situation it

Right
Rebutia kupperiana. Many of the species are easily raised from seed. Not only do the plants themselves produce this freely but it germinates quickly. Sometimes you will find seedlings growing round the parent plant. The flowers remain for about a week and close at night.

Below left
Vriesia splendens and *Aloe aristata*. Many plants grown for the beauty, shape and texture of their foliage also produce attractive flowers. Here, the spikey inflorescence of the vriesia is seen contrasting with the pendent flowers of the aloe. Vriesias are bromeliads, and aloes are leaf succulents which often produce growth in winter and should also produce frequent offsets.

Below right
Epiphyllum ackermannii. This particular plant which itself produces gorgeous showy flowers is the parent of many other handsome hybrids. These have a delightful colour range and beautiful blooms. See also pages 19 and 48.

Far right
Chamaecereus silvestrii is known also as the pea-nut cactus and the prostrate cereus. It is usually happy in a sunny position where it will produce two-inch-long flowers from May to July.

will produce several new shoots quite quickly. If this happens, take the hint and let it remain in its new home. Because of their tall, spiky outlines, sansevierias look well in arrangements.

Another member of the same family, *Aloe variegata*, sometimes called the partridge plant because of its bird-like bars and dots, is also easy. It is often to be seen in windows and although it will grow in sunshine it will also flourish in a shady window, if this is not a contradiction in terms. This aloe also is succulent.

This term – succulent – is used to describe a plant and it is also the term for particular types of plants. Cacti are succulent by nature and also botanically. These are very easy plants to grow and once you have coaxed a cactus into flower it will continue to bloom each year. Some have some very gorgeous blooms, others are small and even dowdy but what they lack in flower power they tend to make up for in plant form and texture. Cacti do not produce leaves. They have plant bodies. Unless they are very fine specimens, cacti do not create a striking decorative effect if they are just stood about in little pots. On the other hand, they do lend themselves well to all kinds of massing and grouping, as we shall see. They are not suitable for mixing with other plants since their water requirements differ.

There are three distinct tribes of cacti. Those in Tribe 1, the pereskieae, are not usually of interest to the house plant collector. Tribe 2 contains most of those we see on sale and which are so good for grouping and for filling bowls and dish gardens. Tribe 3 contains the cereus or night-blooming cacti. Among the loveliest of all, and certainly the most decorative for indoors, are the epiphytic species known loosely as epiphyllums or leaf-flowering cacti. The latter name is really a misnomer because the flowers are not produced on leaves but on flattened stems or plant bodies which somewhat resemble leaves. Most people know the vividly coloured, prettily pendent Christmas cactus, which is just one of the many lovely plants in this group. These can be very decorative and well grown they will make really large plants which become smothered with dozens of blooms.

Often cacti and succulents, from several different plant families, are grouped together under the 'Cactus' heading. It is important to understand that not all succulents are cacti.

One non-cactus family, crassulaceae, contains so many lovely succulent plants which are a delight to the

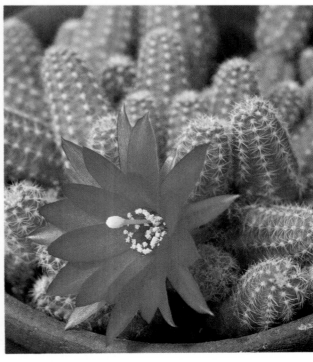

indoor gardener. Their great appeal is that they are beautiful, even when not in bloom. Unlike most cacti, they have no spines. Their leaves are thick, chunky, sometimes wavy-edged, prettily shaped and sometimes gorgeously coloured or perhaps covered with a blue-grey bloom like a grape. Individual plants are often flower-like in form, reminding one of great, thick-petalled roses. Often they are sessile (stemless) and their great rosettes spread out over the soil and out beyond the pot rim. *Aeonium tabulaeforme* is a handsome example. Others in this family carry their plant rosettes on thick, stout trunks and sometimes there will be several rosettes to one stalk. This, like so many in this family, is a good plant for the beginner who will be enchanted with the long well branching flower stem which supports a mass of dainty primrose-coloured flowers.

Many of these succulents produce spectacular flowers, the coral coloured echeveria and the bell-shaped oliveranthus, really an echeveria, are examples. Among this group are the dainty species of crassulas and the fragrant rochea. Some of these closely resemble a kalanchoe and you are likely to find them in bowls of mixed plants which have been assembled and marketed by the florist or nurseryman.

So long as all of these are kept in a temperature of round about 10°C. or 50°F., they will prove to be both easy and rewarding. If you are short of house room they, like cacti, can be stood outdoors for the summer.

Even with the few types we have already discussed, the bromeliads, the lily family succulents, cacti and the crassulas, we have the beginnings of an attractive collection in which there are contrasts of shape, texture, colour and size.

A group of plants which have been standing around indoors, in many countries, for a very long time are the so-called potted palms. These really are tolerant. They will flourish under the most difficult conditions, or so it seems. They must surely be the most undemanding of all of the plants we grow. The palms you are most likely to find on sale are the *Chamaedorea elegans*, a graceful, slow-growing little beauty which is just the right size for many arrangements although it looks very well on its

Right
Unlike most other cacti that can be grown at home, *Aporocactus flagelliformis* has drooping stems, sometimes as long as two feet. As a result it is known as the Rat's tail cactus and it looks well placed on a pedestal or in a hanging basket.

Far right
Rhipsalidopsis gaertneri syn. *Schlumbergera gaertneri.* Revelling in good light, this particular leaf-flowering cactus blooms in spring, hence its popular name, the Easter cactus.

own, especially if it can be silhouetted in some way (this goes for all palms) – you may find this on sale under its synonyms, *Neanthe elegans* or *N. bella* and *Collinia elegans*; *Phoenix dactylifer*, the date palm, sometimes sold as cocos (which it is not, that name belongs to the coconut palm) and perhaps other phoenix species such as *P. roebelinii* and *P. canariensis*, *Butis capitata* whose synonym is *Cocos capitata*; *Howea belmoreana* (synonym *Kentia belmoreana*) the curly palm and *H. fosteriana*, *(K. fosteriana)* the flat or thatch leaf palm, and *Livistone chinensis*, the Chinese fan palm.

So often, when one buys a palm, it seems much too large for its pot and one's first impulse is to repot it to give its roots more living room. However, this would be a mistake, for palms appear to grow best where their roots are restricted. It is possible to keep a plant for as long as two or three years in a 60 pot (3 inch), but plants in such small pots are difficult to deal with and become top heavy. As a temporary expedient plants in too small a pot may be placed, small pot included, in a larger and heavier pot. Pot-bound plants, the term for those whose roots really fill the pots, will require more frequent watering than those with plenty of soil between their roots, which holds more water. For this reason palms and many other plants, as we shall learn, are best plunged, but more of that later.

Palms were at the height of their popularity during the last century during which time two other deep green plants were also much sought after and cherished. One of these was the aspidistra, now rare enough in some countries to be a collector's item. Known then as the

parlour plant and as the cast iron plant it flourished in dim, smoky rooms as well as well-lit surroundings. In summer it was stood outdoors so that its leaves could become cleansed by the summer rains and in winter it went back to its place not so very far from the coal fire. It is a plant which is most difficult to kill. It will send up new leaves in spite of bad treatment, yet if you were to treat it as lovingly as the most precious new plant in your care you would find that it is the ugly duckling among house plants. Grown in good mixture, repotted from time to time, given regular watering and feeding, it gradually turns into a lovely green swan! A good specimen is among the most handsome of all house plants. It will grow high, wide and handsome. A good plant could fill a wide fireplace.

There is a variegated form, *A. elatior* 'Variegata' which, though not quite so robust as the green type, is very attractive. If you find one, keep it in a slightly warmer temperature and in stronger light than the green species but keep it out of direct sunlight.

Probably one of the best known of all our house plants is the so-called rubber plant, *Ficus elastica*, 'Decora', yet it too was a favourite Victorian 'green'. In its natural state this ficus becomes a very tall branching tree but the potted plants are usually grown single-stemmed. The plant grows slowly, a quality, really, in some house plants for once they are in place in the home it is usually most convenient to have them stay in the same position. A good plant should be well clothed with leaves right down to the base of its stem.

It is a jungle plant which means that it can tolerate a

Below
Those who enjoy collecting strange plants often keep a *Stapelia variegata* or some other species of this family of strange succulents which produce fantastic and enormous blooms. Unfortunately some of these have a carrion odour and so the plants cannot always be kept in a much used room.

Far right
Epiphyllum hybrid. One of the many lovely epiphyllums which can be grown indoors. Their colour range is good, from near white through yellow, orange, red, crimson and rose. Their usual height is one to two feet and there are no true leaves – the stems are flattened and look like thick leaves.

good deal of shade—its dark leathery leaves are an indication of this. Plants grown towards the back of the room have better-looking foliage than those which are grown in a sunny place.

There are other species and varieties of ficus which make good house plants although most of them differ in appearance from the rubber plant. Some, like *F. pumila*, are trailers which will cling to a wall if they get the chance and if conditions are right. For instance, if you wished to clothe a wall, stand or plant this ficus near it and keep the wall surface sprayed from time to time. Other ficus have smaller leaves and are more branching in habit than *F. elastica*. *F. benjamina* much resembles a neat citrus tree except, of course, that it does not bear coloured fruits. Mature plants of some of the ficus species do produce little green fruits and you may find them familiar in appearance because ficus is the fig genus or family.

A tall fig is extremely striking in appearance and well deserves the term architectural which is often applied to it. This term is also sometimes used to describe another jungle plant with tough, leathery, deep green leaves, the monstera. While the figs' leaves are simple, those of the monstera are irregular in outline with great slashes and even holes through the leaves. The latter have caused it to be known to some people as the Gruyère cheese plant.

So long as one observes a few simple rules, this handsome plant is easy to grow. It likes a shady position and

Left
Howea belmoreana (syn. *Kentia*). Palms are both decorative and very long-lived. They appear to grow best when their roots are restricted and so they should not be repotted frequently. However, pot bound palms need more water than those which still have plenty of soil between their roots.

Above
Ficus benjamina is just the plant for those who admire the qualities of *F. elastica* (see following page) but not its size or form. Neat, evergreen and prettily branching, it is happiest in rooms where the temperature is never below 50°F (10°C).

Right
The indomitable aspidistra, once so common, is now a rarity in some countries. It will struggle to live in bad conditions, but fed and well cared for it will make a handsome and decorative plant.

it likes to be left to grow in the one place. It likes plenty of pot room and you can always tell when it should be repotted because the leaves become less and less slashed and holed. It is a plant for spacious interiors or for some place where it can roam a wall.

The monstera is botanically allied to philodendron and, as we shall see, there are very many of the arcid family (the Araceae) that make attractive house plants, especially those which like the monstera are climbers. The arum lily is probably the most easily recognised of these. There are several good house plants in this group but not all of them are easy. Many of them flower and some, like the spathiphyllum have white arum-like blooms. Others have green 'arums'. One of the easy and agreeable species is *Syngonium podophyllum* which continues to flourish even under what might be considered to be poor conditions. Like many philodendrons it can be persuaded to grow in water or in sand and water or pebbles and water. As one can appreciate, this facility opens the way to different methods of displaying plants–think, for instance, of the variety of vessels which can then become plant containers. This method of growing will be discussed more fully later on.

Like the bromeliads and the epiphyllums already discussed, philodendrons are also tree growing– epiphytes. Often a new indoor gardener is puzzled by the strange thong-like growths which appear on the stems of some of these plants. These are aerial roots through which the plant takes in moisture from the air, its other kind of roots being used to anchor it to the ground and clinging to the tree on which it grows. When they appear on house plants these roots are best trained down into the soil of the pot.

Of all the philodendrons, *P. scandens*, with deep green heart shaped leaves (because of these it is some-times called sweetheart plant), is possibly the easiest of all to grow. It is also tolerant and can be moved around more than most. Although a climber when given support, it is also a pretty trailer and so is useful in plant arrangements.

Equally tough, in my experience, is a species with much larger leaves, *P. erubescens*, of which there is a form with coppery young leaves known as 'Burgundy'. It is a climber but it grows very slowly and what might appear to be a bushy plant when bought might stay that way for a very long time and then gradually begin to extend its stem and climb.

Also tough is *P. bipinnatifidum*, a non-climbing plant with large feathered leaves of deep, glossy green. These three and others which are on sale, can be grown well back in a room if required.

Where house plants are grown for their decorative qualities, climbing kinds are an essential. Monsteras and certain philodendrons will play this role but there are a few other tough and agreeable plants which also should be considered. Among these are two close relatives to the grape vine, *Cissus antarctica*, which has simple tooth-edged leaves and *Rhoicissus rhomboidea*, which has prettily divided leaves. We shall be meeting these two again.

As one would expect, climbers which also trail are useful to the decorator and if they are also varied in colouration with many hues of green, with white, grey and yellows, they become even more so. The ubiquitous ivies are such plants. The simple, small-leaved green species *Hedera helix* has been a treasured house plant for a long time and it has repaid our love and interest by sporting and producing a remarkable range of different ivies which for convenience sake are known as varieties. So far as easy plants are concerned, here again the old rule proves sound, that the greener the leaf the more tolerant the plant. However, leaf texture also

Above left
Philodendron scandens and *Scindapsus aureus*. Of all the philodendrons, *P. scandens* is possibly the easiest to grow. It trails as prettily as it climbs. The same can be said of scindapsus, although it is a more tender plant which does not tolerate direct sunshine and needs to be kept moist.

Right
Monstera deliciosa in the foreground with a howea by the windows. A large specimen like this will grow in a comparatively small pot for three or four years before needing repotting. When mature, it will produce creamy-coloured spikes which are followed by cone-shaped edible fruits.

Left
Known popularly as the rubber plant, *Ficus elastica* has been a valued house plant for many decades. 'Decora' is an improved cultivar of the original and there are other varieties to be found as well. *F. elastica* can easily grow up to ten feet in a tub if you allow it to.

Following page
Philodendron bipinnatifidum. This particular plant has lived for five years in a room where it receives no direct light. As you can see, its leaves turn towards the main light source. Philodendrons generally are tolerant plants. Keep them warm, fairly humid, but never in bright sunshine.

seems to be of some influence so far as the ivy is concerned and those varieties such as *H. h.* 'Glacier', with small leaves charmingly coloured in grey and white, which have tough textured leaves, as opposed to silky, will tolerate the same dim or away-from-light situations as *H. helix*. On the other hand, large silky-leaved plants such as the cream and green *H. canariensis*, another species altogether, needs a different situation, in good light but not in direct sunlight.

Anyone who hopes to make many plant arrangements throughout the year would do well to build up a stock of varied ivies. These are both cheap to buy and easy to propagate. No other plant, except perhaps the pretty little tradescantia, scrambles so attractively over the edge of a bowl or some other container.

If ivies are given support they will climb. They will also cling, to ceiling or wall should you wish them to do so. If the plants are grown in a tall container or raised from the floor level by some other means, they will also send some of their trails down over the rim and so furnish the lower levels of the container easily and attractively.

As you can see from these few descriptions, house plants vary considerably. As a general rule, the more highly coloured the foliage the more difficult the plant. For example, crotons are perhaps the most gorgeous of all house plants but unless they are grown inside a Wardian glass case or some other enclosed container, a carboy for instance, these will not last for long. Some of the dracaenas have lovely colouration and these also are a little on the temperamental side. Often such plants will grow quite well during the summer months and it is a good plan to introduce them into the home at that time so that they can gradually adapt themselves to their surroundings.

On the other hand, there are some almost hardy garden plants which make good house plants. These could be so useful for those who want some plants for a situation in which it is not possible to provide much warmth, an outer landing to a flat for instance. Ivies, which might take a few weeks to become adjusted if they have been brought from a warm greenhouse, *Araucaria excelsa* or Norfolk Island Pine, fatsia and fatshedera and forms of euonymus are examples.

Far right
Cissus antarctica, popularly called the kangaroo vine, can be grown as a pillar or with its long trails divided to cover a wall. As its specific name indicates, it prefers a cool situation to one which is warm and arid.

Right and Below right
Rhoicissus rhomboidea (the grape ivy) will fit into many places in the home. Here it is climbing well and being encouraged to frame an archway leading from kitchen to dining room. If required, it can be kept neat and bushy by pinching out the tips of its growing stems. It looks attractive placed at the edges of a group or arrangement so that some of its trails can cascade prettily, and will grow well away from direct light.

Flowering plants

Most flowering plants have to be regarded as temporary decorations. Fortunately, they are so extremely beautiful that what they lack in staying power they make up for in colour and general beauty. It is quite natural that most of us should wish to keep them for as long as possible, perhaps to bloom another year, but this is seldom possible.

So many of our flowering plants are annuals, examples are cineraria, exacum, browallia, and once these have flowered they die. There are some flowering kinds which are perennials treated as annuals, which means that they can be brought quickly into bloom but this causes them to expend their energies so freely that they are soon spent once they have flowered.

Other perennials and some shrubs, azaleas and

Left
A November display of cyclamen, begonias and cinerarias. All these plants need careful watering if they are to live any length of time.

Below
Anthurium scherzerianum.
Known as the Piggy-tail plant, because of their curly spadices, these anthuriums are really quite tough house plants. They grow best in good light, without this they will not flower. They dislike draughts and dry conditions.

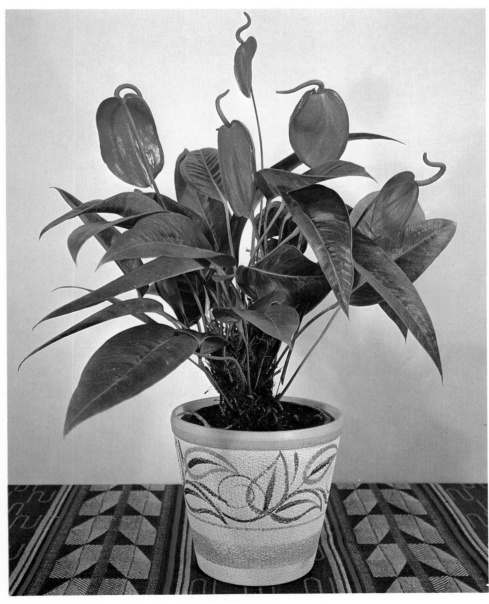

Right
Caladium with Hippeastrum, which is popularly though wrongly called amaryllis, has such spectacular flowers that it is hard to believe that the bulbs are easily grown. It is sometimes possible to buy prepared, ready-potted bulbs which will flower very quickly. Plant the bulbs singly in a loam based compost leaving the top of the bulb exposed and keep moist until the leaves die down.

Opposite page top
A west-facing window is an ideal spot in which to grow an assortment of plants. Among these flowering here are an epiphyllum hybrid, an Easter cactus and the dark-leaved *Impatiens walleriana petersiana*. Impatiens are shrubby semi-succulent plants which have clusters of bright flowers. Some of them are perennials and tip cuttings can be taken at any time.

Below right
Hyacinths will grow in water alone with a nugget of charcoal put at the bottom to keep the water sweet. There are special glasses made to hold the bulbs. A little grass sprinkled over the soil surface furnishes a simple flower pot. Crocuses, scillas and most small-flowering bulbs should not be brought indoors until the buds are ready to open.

Below far right
Many lilies can be grown quite well in pots of soil like any other bulbs. There are some, like this midcentury hybrid, 'Enchantment' which may be sold ready potted and prepared to flower quickly with the minimum of attention.

heaths (*Erica*), are subjected to even more severe methods of cultivation and by various means are forced into bloom completely out of their natural season. It is not the purpose of this book to explain these processes but it is important that I should point out that should such a plant continue to live after it has finished flowering it is most unlikely to produce flowers again in the following year in the same season. Usually, such plants take two or three years to become adjusted. Poinsettias are the best known examples.

On the other hand there are many other much more permanent plants which flower prettily and for more than one year at a time. Some, like saintpaulia or African violets may flower more than once a year.

Some of these may be grown for their flowers alone, their leaves being unremarkable and the plants themselves not highly decorative except when in bloom. There are also many foliage plants which reward one with the odd flower or two. As I described earlier, aechmeas and some other bromeliads produce unusual flowers which are extremely decorative and long lasting, others are more interesting than decorative. The same applies to aroids: anthurium and spathiphyllum produce showy blooms but others may be green and leaf-like.

Lovely flowering plants which present few problems are those which are grown from bulbs. These can be bought in pots and bowls already planted and in bud or bloom. Alternatively, the indoor gardener can grow them from the very beginning. The bulb is planted in bulb fibre, soil, water or water and pebbles – according to its kind. If the bulb has to be forced into flower out of season, it is usually expendable for it will not flower in the same way nor at the same time the following year. Often forced bulbs of hardy plants, hyacinths, tulips and daffodils, for instance, can be planted in the garden and there they will gradually recuperate and bloom again one day.

Some bulbous plants are perennial indoors in the sense that they can be saved and grown again year after year. Often these have to be rested which means that they remain in their pots but are not watered. When the time comes they are repotted, watered and started into growth again. Hippeastrums, sometimes called amaryllis, hymenocallis, sprekelia, lapeyrousia and nerines are examples and all of these can be bought easily from bulb merchants.

More and more kinds of bulbs are being marketed ready planted but not grown. These bulbs have also

29

been specially prepared and their cultivation is simplicity itself. The gardener is so well rewarded for the minimum of effort, one simply follows the bulb merchant's instructions. Often there is nothing to do but to water the pot and stand it in good light and soon there are gorgeous hippeastrums, lilies, lilies-of-the-valley, tulips, narcissi, hyacinths or colchicums to admire. All is astonishingly easy. New types of bulbs which can be grown this way are being introduced annually. It is also possible to buy prepared bulbs of certain kinds of flowers and to plant these yourself.

Whatever group flowering plants might fall into generally speaking there are a few rules which apply to all. Except for a very few kinds, spathiphyllum, a shade lover is an example, plants in bloom need good light though not, as has been stressed already, direct sunlight which might scorch them.

If the plant is not highly decorative when not in flower, you might find it convenient to move it around and to keep it in some less obvious place until its flower buds show. However, do choose the new site with care.

You can tell if a plant is not getting enough light because its stems become drawn and floppy and its flowers are not as well coloured as they should be. We shall discuss the influence of light on plants more fully later. Obviously, if you notice signs you should take action. Conversely, if you notice the blooms on a plant have suddenly flopped, even petals clinging together instead of being wide apart, you should move the plant to a less sunny place, for the time being at least. If you have no other site but a sunny windowsill, hang a fine curtain between the glass and the plant.

However, it may not be light alone which is causing the trouble. Water and humidity are also essential to flowering plants and at times, lack of these two may be critical.

One group of flowering plants which seems to do best in a really sunny window and in a dry atmosphere is the pelargonium, popularly called geranium. Although they are more often grown outdoors in windowboxes and hanging baskets than in the home, they are in fact good decorative house plants. They must have good light. Sometimes in summer a plant in a very hot and sunny situation will loose too much water and droop its leaves and should this happen it should either be given a larger pot or moved to some other place. The plants produce flowers intermittently throughout winter, even those which have been grown outdoors and are

This page
The commercial grower can induce chrysanthemums to flower all year round. He can also dwarf them to make compact and floriferous pot plants. Like most flowering plants, and the berried solanums with them here, they need good light.

Right
Some of the most popular gift plants. Of these the azalea and heaths should be kept constantly moist at the roots. Primulas and chrysanthemums need cool situations if they are to last well. *Solanum capsicastrum* and a prettily variegated ivy complete the picture.

brought in for decoration during the winter months.

Azaleas and heathers should never be allowed to dry out and are always best plunged. Feed these fortnightly when they are in bud and water them with rain water.

Cinerarias are among the very few plants which do best if they are watered every day. Certainly, they should never be allowed to become dry at the roots for once these plants wilt they will never properly revive.

Becoming almost dry at the roots does not harm some plants as much as one might expect. Indeed, the aeration caused by the rushing of the water through the dry soil and out through the pot is beneficial to the roots, but this does not apply to many flowering kinds.

Other plants which, like cinerarias need watering and feeding liberally are calceolarias. These need a warmer temperature than the foregoing but like them they need really good light.

The many little pot chrysanthemums now on sale, usually dwarf and very compact and grown under intense scientific cultivation, are often found to have small pots packed full of roots. This being the case, the plants need plenty of water. In a warm room, perhaps

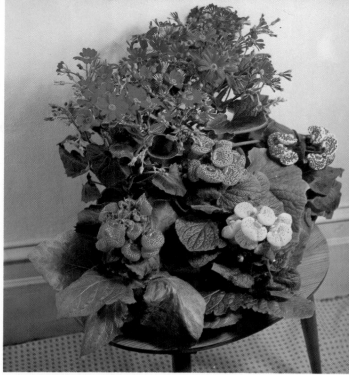

Left
Primulas are attractive flowering plants and there are a number of different species: the large-flowered *Primula obconica* and the daintier *P. malacoides* are probably the best known. They like plenty of water and light feeding when in flower. Plants may be raised from seed quite easily. Also in the picture is a standard azalea, a sansevieria and a small-leaved ivy.

Top right
Vividly coloured cinerarias and calceolarias will last longer and produce more blooms if they are watered liberally and fed whilst in flower. There are many lovely varieties of both kinds of plants in a gorgeous range of colours.

Right
Hydrangeas are an exception to the general rule and are among the few flowering house plants which do best in some shade. If they are stood in full sunlight they are likely to flag too badly ever to be fully revived to their former brilliance.

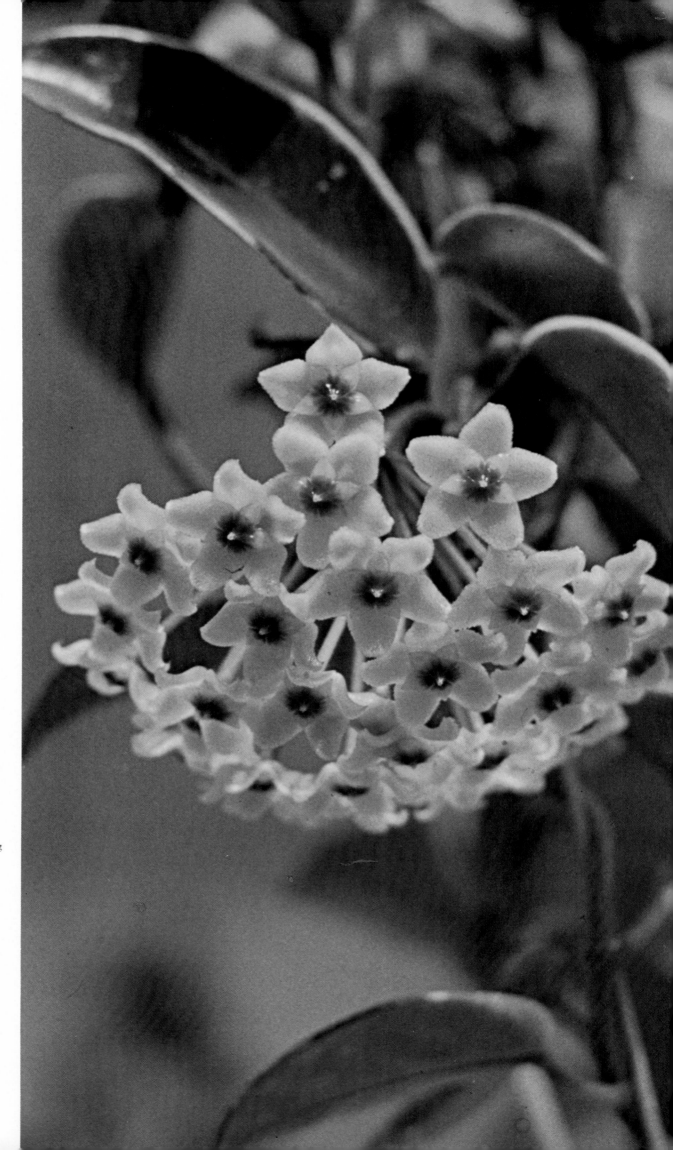

Right
Hoya carnosa. There is also
a charming variegated variety
of this plant as well as the
green-leaved *H. bella* which
produces even more brilliant
wax-flowers, as they are called.
A climber, the hoya is a little
slow in beginning, but speedy
once established.

Opposite above
A group of three flowering
plants showing greatly differing
'blooms'. The 'rat tails' are
the flowers of *Peperomia
glabella*, on the left are the red
piggy tails of an anthurium,
and behind are the vivid blue
flowers of browallia, which is
an annual and easily raised
from seed. Peperomias like a
humid atmosphere and the pot
soil should be kept fairly dry
in winter.

Opposite below
Some ornamental-leaved
begonias flower prettily, like
this *Begonia haageana.* There
are many species and varieties
which will grow well, even
luxuriantly, indoors so long as
they have warmth and some
humidity.

34

daily. If there are still many buds to open it is also wise to feed them weekly because the plant foods become leached out by so much water.

Hydrangeas need much the same treatment. These are among the few flowering plants which do best away from strong light.

Solanum capsicastrum the winter cherry and the kinds of pot peppers, capsicum, need very careful watering if they are not to drop their buds and leaves. These grow best when they also can be sprayed daily. Like cyclamen, they prefer a cool atmosphere and good light. While they are in bud, bloom and fruit, they should be fed weekly.

Cyclamen should be watered from the base—the water should be poured into the saucer or whatever other vessel the pot stands in. Better still, they should be plunged. Always avoid pouring water over the corm because droplets tend to rest between the bases of the stems and these cause the corm to rot. One great cause of cyclamen dying apart from incorrect watering are fumes of gas, oil, smoke, paint and others in the atmosphere. Keep them cool, never in a warm room.

Many plants appreciate a little moisture sprinkled or sprayed over their foliage and this is best done in the early morning but not when the sun is shining on the leaves, the reason for this being that droplets can cause diseases to take hold.

Primula obconica and *P. sinensis* seem to do best when they are moistened in this way and I think that it helps any type of these of plants grown indoors, especially any lifted from the garden.

It is not generally known that the garden primroses and polyanthus can be grown in pots on a windowsill in good light. These should be potted in J.I. potting compost in autumn or at any time during winter. If you have no garden, buy garden plants and pot them yourself if they are not being sold already potted.

Most primulas will grow indoors but some are better than others as house plants. *P. kewensis* has fragrant yellow flowers in clusters on tall stems.

Speaking generally, those just mentioned can be grouped as temporary plants and with them the many others that I may not yet have mentioned simply because there is always a continually changing supply of annual flowering plants on the market which may include exacum and browallia, besides some which have vivid foliage such as coleus.

So far as the perennials are concerned, there are people who manage to keep these from one year to the next—an operation which is simplified if one has a greenhouse or conservatory. Azaleas, cyclamen and solanums, for instance, can be kept outdoors, the pots sunk or plunged in garden soil in some partially shaded place. Those who have no gardens sometimes keep the plants on a shady outer windowsill or even indoors in a cool shaded window. At the end of summer the plants are brought indoors or, in the case of those already there, given a little more attention, extra food and water. The azaleas should be repotted in pure peat, well rammed down, after flowering, solanums when they are brought in for the winter and cyclamen corms when they have died down.

Among those flowering plants which are temporary or semi-permanent, according to the skill of the gardeners, are some which are grown from tubers, for example, achimenes, begonias, gloxinias (*sinningia* botanically) and the handsome caladiums which are grown for their colourful leaves and are gorgeous enough to be classed as flowers in this case.

Some begonias do not make tubers and are fibrous-rooted and some of these are also known as winter-flowering begonias.

Many of the flowering plants we shall discuss more fully when we deal with plant arrangements and pot-et-fleur, but just a few words about a special few.

Most columnea species available are beautiful trailing plants with long green-leaved stems which become studded with scarlet-orange flowers.

Euphorbias are varied and the showy poinsettia is one of this family but there are others which resemble cactus plants. Poinsettias are inclined to be temperamental. They dislike too warm rooms, fumes of any sort, draughts either hot or cold and direct sunshine. Their roots should be kept constantly moist and the plant is best plunged. Gardenias, again, are not easy because they need humidity. In some ways it is more important to spray the foliage than to water the soil. Gloxinias, like cyclamen should be watered from below. They need airy not close surroundings but no draughts. *Hoya carnosa*, a pretty little thick-leaved climber is most often sold with its trails trained round in a hoop resting on the rim of the pot. You can unwind these stems and treat the plant like any other climber if you wish but it will go on round and round the hoop if you prefer it that way. This plant must have warmth. Hypocyrta, known as the goldfish plant because of the shape and colour of its little flowers is quite tough and can be grown in a not-so-warm room.

Impatiens or busy lizzie, a great favourite, often appears to thrive in spite of its owners and its surroundings. A well-grown plant should be smothered in flowers. Keep the tips of the shoots pinched out to keep the plant bushy. Feed it when it is in bloom. Keep it warm in winter. Saintpaulia or African violet often fails because of bad light, polluted atmosphere and low temperatures. It grows best when plunged and a bowl or trough of mixed varieties can look very attractive indeed.

Among the bulbous plants you can expect to grow all year round, as opposed to those which have to be planted in the autumn and forced into bloom are the following: clivia with handsome strap-like leaves, haemanthus or blood lily, hippeastrum or amaryllis, hymenocallis, nerine, oxalis, vallota and velthemia.

Below
Euphorbia pulcherrima. Known universally as the poinsettia, this is the most flamboyant member of the spurge family. The vividly coloured bracts surround the tiny berry-like flowers. To keep the colour (red, pink or cream), give the plants plenty of light at all times, but not direct sunlight.

Right
Saintpaulia ionantha 'Diana Blue'. There are many named varieties and some good strains of African violets now available. If you are successful in growing them you will find that they are also easy plants to propagate. They like good light, clean air, humidity and feeding when in flower.

How to choose your plants

Few of us have an opportunity of buying direct from the nursery. Those who live in cities have to buy from a florist or perhaps a garden centre and this means that the plants have left the nursery, travelled to market and been sold there either by the grower's salesman or by a wholesale florist. The retail florist has to buy the plants from the market, transport them to his own establishment and there, finally, place them on show for your selection. Obviously, there have been several opportunities for some harm to come to the plant and with the best will in the world it is not always possible for the retail florist to keep a close enough eye on each of his many plants to ensure that they are always in the best of condition. Furthermore, not all florists are horticulturists and may not recognise that a plant is suffering or is likely to do so.

So far as flowering plants are concerned, our method of marketing means that there is unlikely to be sufficient time for any of the blooms to have passed their peak and be on the way out. Most have some blooms and plenty of buds still to come which is what you should look for. Should you be offered any plant on which it is obvious that even one flower is fading treat it a little suspiciously and select another if you can. Watch out for fading blooms and for those which are flagging or wilting. This may be caused only by thirst and if the plant has been dry only for a short period no harm is done and the situation is soon rectified, but flagging can also be caused through draughts and severe cold. A good guide is to buy plants and flowers rather in the same way as one chooses salad vegetables. Look primarily for crispness and colour. Whether the plant you seek bears flowers or whether it is grown for the beauty of its foliage, a healthy plant has a certain crisp appearance about it. Stems are turgid, stiff, not limp or drooping, even if it should be a trailing kind. Colour should be deep and glowing, leaves should gleam. Be suspicious of any plant which seems faded in appearance. Certain leaves have a metallic sheen on them which is more intensified when they are in the pink of condition. Hairy leaves should look new-brushed and not shabby.

Accept nothing that has spots on it, that is, unnatural spots which are obviously the result of burning or disease. The tissues of these spots will be drier than the main leaf fabric or blistery in appearance. There may be only one spot on a leaf or there may be several. Test the spot by merely wiping the leaf gently between the finger and thumb. Some green plants have a slight deposit caused by the water with which they have been sprayed, particularly if it is limy, but this is easily smoothed away and does no damage.

Some leaves may appear to have a dried brown edging to them. Do not accept a young plant in a small pot in this condition for this is usually an indication of a damaged or sick leaf. However, should the plant be a handsome specimen with very many leaves, begonias

Left
Beloperone guttata. The brownish-rose flowers give this plant its common name of shrimp plant. Although it grows best with some warmth and humidity, cooler and dryer conditions tend to deepen the colour of the attractive bracts. Feed moderately, particularly when in flower.

39

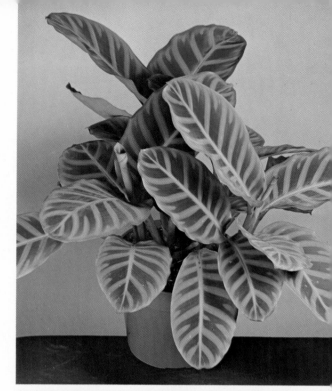

are examples, it might be that one or two of the older, that is the first formed leaves, are on their way out, as might be expected. They still have a role to play for leaves are the lungs of a plant, its stomach too for that matter, and it is unwise to cut away any leaf while it still has life for it continues to contribute to the well being of the plant and is part of its metabolic system.

A plant should fill its pot. Be suspicious of a plant whose pot looks too large for it. Ailing leaves may have been cut away.

Always examine the growing tips or shoots to make sure that they are sturdy, plump, healthy and capable of further growth. Buds should be succulent. Pointed tips as in philodendrons should be well filled. If they are papery they probably do not contain a living shoot and this indicates that the plant was neglected at some time. There might be future trouble in store. Papery buds do not contain flowers. See that buds are all alike. If you are examining a flowering plant check that there are many more buds to come. If you buy a plant with all its blooms open wide then expect it to be at its best for a short period only.

Whether the plant is a temporary or permanent kind always treat yellowing leaves with suspicion, unless, of course, they are supposed to have some yellow variation in them. Usually, the leaf of a green plant yellows because of ill health and there is a change of texture too. The leaf becomes less tough, sometimes even pappy to the touch. Several yellowing leaves on ivy, cyclamen, from bulbs and others, usually indicate that either the plants are older than they ought to be or very sick, though one leaf may, as has already been suggested, merely be a spent leaf and is no cause for worry.

As I said earlier, a pot should be well filled. Unless stems are naturally leafless, such as those of cyperus which produces little umbrella like topknots, the foliage should always persist to the base. This need not necessarily be thick and bushy but it should be healthy. Plants without tall main stems, such as saintpaulias and begonias should have full crowns. They should fill the pot so well that they cover its rim.

Plants like solanums or winter cherries, heaths and azaleas, all entirely different kinds of plants, show distress by shedding their leaves. One or two only may drop but sometimes these one or two are the beginning of a real fall. If when you are choosing a plant, on the soil surface you see a leaf, or in the case of heaths, some needles do not buy the plant, unless its length of life is really of no consequence. This leaf drop can be caused by more than one factor, drought, draught or insect pests.

So far as size is concerned, all tastes are catered for. Small pots are useful for making plant arrangements and pot-et-fleur. Climbers and plants which are required to stand in a certain place in the home and to act rather as a piece of furniture are best bought in a large pot so that they need never be repotted. The most popular size of pot plant is a 60 or 3 inch, measured across the rim, but there is a large 60 and a small 60. Take care when buying containers that size is taken into account or you will be left with a misfit. It is surprising to discover, as one does, that most 'cover' pots have been designed and made without reference to flower pot sizes. Unless they are arranged and plunged into some moisture retentive medium, small pots are apt to dry out rather quickly once they carry a lot of growth. However, as we shall learn, there are ways of avoiding this. A plant in a 48, the 5 inch pot, is usually about twice the price of the same plant in a 60. Incidentally, pots came by these odd terms because of the way clay pots were made, so many in a cast.

Many flowering plants are sold in 60s and these are

Above right
Calathea zebrina. Closely related to the marantas, calatheas like warmth and humidity. Plants grow best plunged in moist peat inside a larger waterproof pot. They should be kept out of direct sunlight.

Above centre
Crocus chrysanthus 'Princess Beatrix'. All bulbs are safe buys and their successful flowering depends on the conditions and treatment. Crocuses are more difficult than some other bulbs to grow indoors – hyacinths are the easiest for the beginner (see pages 102, 106 for planting instructions)

Far right
Citrus mitis is a rewarding plant to keep at home since it will flower and fruit when young and nearly all the year round. The leathery green leaves quickly indicate if the plant is not healthy by turning yellow.

Right
Gloxinia. With a little planning these flowers can be enjoyed during many months of the year. They can be raised from seed and from cuttings of stem or leaves. The plants form tubers which can be saved from year to year.

African violets, *Saintpaulia ionantha*, are very varied and come in colours ranging from white through pink, rose, purple, violet and blue. These are beautiful flowers from a healthy plant: their colour is good, there are plenty of buds, the hairy leaves and stems are stiff and well brushed.

Left
Philodendron scandens and *Philodendron ilsemanii*. The many pointed tips of *Philodendron scandens* are well filled and the leaves glossy and healthy. Leaves of all plants should be kept free of dust if they are to remain healthy and attractive. Regular sponging with clean luke-warm water keeps them shiny.

Right
Nidularium fulgens. This is a useful plant to have around because it is tolerant and can be moved to fill any odd corner or to make a glowing focal point to an arrangement or group of plants. It is a bromeliad and so easy to water – simply keep the central zone always filled. The leaves should be dark and glossy and they grow up to 12 inches long.

Right
Rhododendron simsii. Among the most popular of all flowering house plants, and better known as azaleas, they should be regarded as temporary tenants. More azaleas die of drought than from any other cause, since the root ball must never become dry.

Below
Cyclamen are such popular house plants and there are so many in all florists, particularly around Christmas, that it is important to choose these plants with great care. Check that no leaves show signs of being at all unhealthy and that there are flower buds to come. Many plants are brought on too quickly before they are sold and are consequently difficult to keep.

Far right
Primula obconica is a winter blooming primrose which you can keep from year to year. The colour range is very wide, and again when choosing a plant check that there are plenty of buds to come and that the leaves are a fresh green in colour with their stems firm and upstanding.

Centre right
A really healthy African violet produces flowers which glow strongly with colour.

Below right
Aphelandra squarrosa is a most attractive plant to have in the home. The flowers provide a striking contrast to the dark green banded leaves. Keep the atmosphere moist in summer.

very useful for plant arrangements for they can be treated a little like a bunch of flowers and replaced when they have passed their best.

Azaleas and ericas or heaths are peat-loving and so are potted in peat. This can create problems. If the peat, which is very porous, is allowed to become dry, it shrinks. If the root ball is allowed to remain dry it shrinks and pulls away from the sides of the pot. It is possible to soak the plant and so recharge it but sometimes the drying has gone so far that the re-soaked plant is never the same again. Look at the lower portion of the stalk or little trunk. This should always be moist and darker than the wood above it. When you have the plant at home, keep it this way and then you will know that the roots are moist enough.

If you buy plants for gifts, do not collect them too much in advance of the date when you want to give them. Certainly order these well in advance. If you take the plants home too soon, they will begin to adjust to your own home conditions and then when you pass them on to another home they will have to begin all over again and they may sulk. Your gift will then not be as acceptable as you had hoped.

Never leave plants wrapped. Wrap the plants at the last moment if you must. If you are going by car and the weather is fine you can take plants unwrapped. Otherwise, the best thing is to slip each plant inside a large clear plastic bag so that it is entirely enveloped. Blow into the bag to inflate it so that the plastic stands well away from the leaves and flowers and fasten the top securely. Be generous and use a large bag so that when it is pulled off it does not brush against the plant itself.

Guard against the plant falling over or about. Quite often the best way to secure it is to take a cardboard box, turn it upside down and pierce the centre. From this hole make a few incisions, short or long according to the size of the container and press the pot down into the space thus made open. Allow about two thirds of the pot to go down into the box. The plant will then be elevated and out of harm's way and it will then be possible to push heavy objects against the sides of the box to prevent it moving. Another method, and this is good for small plants, is to fit a box or tray with a block of Oasis foam and to press the pot into this.

If the weather is really cold when you buy plants, avoid street stalls and ignore any plants put on show in the open air. They are likely to succumb later. Always insist on having the whole plant you buy covered and not just the pot. If you can have it slipped into a plastic bag so much the better.

Nurserymen tend to concentrate on those plants which are good do-ers, as you can appreciate. Not only must they grow well but travel well also. A plant must look as well on sale as it did in the nursery. This means that some plants are hard to find, the easy-going plectranthus which is somewhat too brittle to market, is an example. Such plants can often be found at small nurseries, market stalls and horticultural societies' stalls.

Growing hints

Many plants die because they have been given too much water and this means that they, or part of them, drown. When there is too much water in the soil, roots die because they cannot breathe. Roots need air as well as moisture. Unless a plant's roots are happy and growing well it will not be able to function properly above soil level. It is always best to err on keeping a plant a little on the dry side than to allow the soil to remain constantly moist—unless the plant is one which likes a boggy condition, a cyperus is an example.

It may appear to be paradoxical that although the greatest danger to indoor plants is drowning by over-watering, it is nevertheless possible to strike cuttings by placing shoots in water and it is also possible to grow certain plants in water alone.

One famous producer of house plants has recently developed a system known under the trade name of hydroculture or hydroponic cultivation where certain plants are grown without soil and with water and special

Right
Plants sometimes need to be—and can be—kept under control. The Hoya at the back of the group, instead of being allowed to climb, has been trained round a hoop. The trailing plectranthus has been kept in a small pot to constrict its growth and the striped cryptanthus has been left to grow into a cluster.

Far right
Caladium hybrids. Caladiums are among the few foliage plants that are very difficult to grow. They rarely survive the winter outside a green-house. They grow from tubers and require plenty of warmth and water while they are growing freely.

fertilizer alone. The pots in which they are grown are designed to indicate the water level and the plants themselves have their roots anchored in marble-size pellets of baked clay which absorb a certain amount of moisture yet allow plenty of space between them for air. There is also a facility for administering a special long-lasting fertilizer. All this means that the initial cost of plants grown in these containers must necessarily be high, but on the other hand for the first time ever in horticulture, so far as I am aware, the growers offer a six month guarantee of the plant.

Yet it is a simple matter to grow some plants in water alone at minimal cost and for several years without special containers, anchoring pellets, water level indicators or fertilizers. The main principle, as

with the hydroculture method, is to permit the roots to obtain both air and moisture. The hydroculture method makes use of the clay granules for the roots to anchor the plant, much as do the pebbles in the puddle pot system described on page 100 and pictured on pp. 108 and 109, but so long as the plant is securely anchored at the top of the container with wire netting or some similar device they are quite unnecessary.

The hydroculture method embodies a permanent indicator of the water level, but if a clear glass container is used it is always possible to check this at a glance. The simplest way to make sure that the roots obtain both moisture and air is to allow the water level to drop to, say, the half-way mark before topping up again. In summer this will normally take ten days or so, in winter up to a month. The roots will be found to develop so that some reach down into the water and so provide moisture at all times, while others stay nearer to the neck of the container so that at most times they can breathe air. Because there is a danger of the accumulation of fertilizer in the water if normal doses are given it is wise with this growing method to halve quantities used for the feeding programme.

As soon as a plant comes into your hands see if it needs water. The simplest test of all is to take a scrap of newspaper and with the thumb press it on the soil surface. If the soil is moist enough the paper will immediately become damp. Another method is to weigh the pot in your hand. A pot filled with damp soil is heavier than one in which there is dry soil. If the pot is made of clay and not plastic you can rap it with a pencil or some other object. A pot of dry soil will ring, a pot of moist or wet soil will give a dull sound. You will get to know simply by looking at the plant whether or not it is needing a drink.

If you find that the plant is dry, take a bucket or a bowl or if you have several plants use the sink, but see that the water level will come above the rim of the pot. Plunge carefully and watch for a stream of bubbles which should rise from the soil to the surface of the water. Wait until the stream of bubbles stops. Take out the pot plant and stand it on the draining board or in the sink and clean the outside of the pot. Leave the plant to drain.

From this time on, how often any plant will need watering will depend entirely upon the plant itself and its surroundings. Usually a flowering plant will need more than one which has large leaves only. Test, as suggested, by pressing with newspaper.

Although most house plants need a certain amount of warmth, central heating is not good for them unless this can be tempered by humidity. It helps tremendously if you can spray the air round a plant and sometimes its foliage also with clean water from an atomiser. Use rain water both for watering and spraying if possible. This is essential if the mains water contains lime and you are growing azaleas and other lime haters.

Fortunately, there is a method of providing humidity which also improves the general appearance and consequently the decorative value of the pot plant as well. This involves plunging the plant pot inside a larger cover pot. All kinds of vessels can be used for this purpose. Flower vases, especially those with a stem or short pedestal base are ideal because they lift and display the plants so attractively. Most bromeliads, which are inclined to be top heavy sometimes, look well in the urn-type, classic flower vase. Pedestal vases are invaluable where a spreading plant is growing in a small flower pot. Unprotected or un-anchored it is likely to become easily knocked over.

But to return to the actual plunging. In any of these cover pots—and the term extends to troughs and other

Right
Epiphyllum hybrid. One of the many lovely flowering cacti known as leaf-flowering—a misnomer because the flowers are really produced on the flattened stems or plant bodies. The main flowering period is from May to June.

Opposite page top
Dieffenbachia picta. There are several species of this plant. They like warm, humid, light conditions but will become adapted to cooler, dryer environments. Stem portions and sap are highly poisonous to humans causing swollen mouth membranes, hence the popular name Dumb Cane.

Opposite page bottom
Watering bromeliads is quite a different operation from caring for other plants. In their case it is important that the little well, vase or reservoir at the heart of the plant and made by the overlapping leaves is always kept filled with water.

large containers, you should pack well-moistened peat, bulb-fibre, sand, moss, old crumbled Oasis which you have used for flower arrangements, vermiculite or any clean water-retentive material you can find, including, if all else fails, shredded kitchen paper. This packing should go under and around the pot plant, reaching right up to the rim which should be well below the edge of the outer pot, to make watering clean and easy.

The packing or plunge material should be kept moist but not sodden. If you use this method you will find that plants grow better, even though you do not have to water them so frequently, than if they are simply stood on a saucer with the surface of the pot exposed to the drying air. Cacti should not be in a moist plunge but some succulents, especially the epiphytic kinds, benefit from it. Several different kinds of plants can be mixed together in a plunge medium but we will discuss this more fully when we come to the subject of plant arrangement generally.

Although plants help to cleanse our atmosphere for us, taking in the gases we cannot use and expelling precious oxygen, they or at least some of them can become badly affected by some atmospheric conditions. Fumes from oil lamps and heaters, from manufactured gas appliances, from paint, cleaning fluids, even tobacco can affect some so much that they become ill or even die. Saintpaulias, pelargoniums and cyclamen are examples. Generally speaking, once again, the dark green tough-leaved kinds are best able to tolerate pollution and those with thick chunky leaves or plant bodies such as sansevierias and cacti seldom show signs of distress.

Unfortunately, we find that just as plants become over-watered so do many of them become over-fed. One should certainly feed plants from time to time but never too generously. Too much plant food can kill so never be tempted to give just a little more. Plants producing flower buds, or those which have been rested and are coming into growth again, usually need feeding but generally speaking they need only sufficient food to keep them healthy and of good appearance. As a rule, it is much more convenient for a permanent plant to grow slowly. Plants which grow too fast and consequently too large, can be a nuisance. You have to find new homes for them. By feeding a plant very lightly we can keep it growing in proportion with its environment and to the purpose for which we chose it. It will thrive – but slowly.

We should always remember that plants in our homes are influenced by the amount of artificial light and extra warmth around them and so they cannot be expected to behave as they would if they were growing naturally. All plants rest at some time of the year but this period of rest may not necessarily be in winter or, if this is the proper time for the plant to take its rest, growth might continue because artificial light extends the length of the plant's day.

It is not difficult to tell whether or not a plant is making new growth. If it is winter and you see no signs of this, do not feed the plant but allow it to rest instead. Usually, during these rest periods, you will find that plants need less water also. As soon as you see signs of new growth you will find that a little more water is needed and once this happens you can give the plant a little help by feeding it with a very little soluble plant food. It is best to start very gently by putting just a little in the regular water and then you can lead up to maximum amounts should these be necessary, tapering off again when you feel that the plant is slowing down.

Plant care

Plants that are unhealthy cannot remain decorative for long and so it follows that if we want them to give us full value we should learn how to care for them when they are healthy and how to tend them when they are ailing in some way or other.

First of all let us make quite sure that we all know what is meant by watering a plant. This does not mean pouring a tablespoonful over the surface each morning nor does it mean allowing a pot to stand in several inches of water for some hours.

In every pot, bowl or other container, there should be a free area between the top soil or soil surface and the brim, rim or edge. Thinking in terms of the flower pots themselves, this space should be between a ½–1 inch for a 60, and for a 48 more, because more water is needed for a larger plant. Bear these points in mind when you repot plants or make dish gardens or plant other types of containers—you need room to water.

When the plant is watered this area should be filled. If the soil compost is properly mixed and well-drained or open as it should be, and certainly if the soil is dry, the water will be quickly sucked through and, if the plant should be standing in a saucer, you will notice that this quickly fills. This water should not be tipped away but should be left so that the soil and roots can slowly absorb it. If the pot soil is already wet enough the water takes longer to drain through. This may be an indication that you are watering too much or too often. Should this be the case, you can apply a little first aid by standing the pot on some absorbent material, several folds of newspaper for example, so that moisture is drawn out. Allow the soil to become almost quite dry before you water the plant again. Plants which are plunged lose their water into the plunge material and are able to re-absorb it slowly.

Plants in flower are at their peak and usually they need more water at this time. If they are in bud when you buy them, or if you have them young and so watch them come into bud, they should be fed. As we have already learned, plants need humidity and one should remember that a plant in flower has an even greater surface through which precious moisture will be lost if the atmosphere is too dry. If your plants are plunged you may have to water them a little more often than usual, so it is wise to check. Use an atomiser on the plants but keep the spray off the actual flowers in case these are the kind that become discoloured. If your plants are newly bought and are labelled, you may be advised to water freely. It is difficult for me to say just how often this might be necessary because this depends upon the size of the plant, the number of its blooms and where it stands. It might need no more than a weekly watering, on the other hand, some flowering plants in

Left
Aphelandra, begonia and variegated hibiscus. These and many other plants need a high degree of humidity in the home. They are best grown with their pots plunged inside another filled with some moisture-retentive material such as peat. The aphelandra is a beautiful plant; the leaves can be up to ten inches long and it has large yellow flowers set in vase shaped bracts.

Below
Maranta leuconeura. 'Erythrophylla'. Marantas need a warm, moist atmosphere or they will not produce a succession of new leaves. A gentle spray of clean water on the foliage from time to time will help to keep them happy.

hot sunny weather, need watering every day.

Some people let the plant pot stand in a puddle of water in a saucer and although this might work sometimes it is not really to be recommended. The soil seldom becomes aerated this way and it is possible for it to become so water-logged that the plant finally dies. Plants should 'paddle' only when directions for their culture include the advice, 'keep the soil constantly moist'. An example is the little flowering rush-like *Cyperus*.

It is important to clean plants so that their leaf pores do not become clogged with dust. If it is convenient, stand plants outdoors in a gentle summer shower but guard against wind and torrential rains because these could damage the leaves. If you can spray climbing and large leaved plants in situ, so much the better. To avoid making the soil too wet if you do this, spread a little plastic or a dust sheet over the pot surface.

If leaves have become very dusty one must guard against scratching them with any grit particles which might be in the dust. The best way to clean a really dusty plant is to syringe it so that the dust is washed away. It is possible sometimes to blow the dust by using a vacuum cleaner in reverse, in which case one has to work quickly to suck the dust in from the air immediately after this. Alternatively, carefully sponge the leaves with a sponge, soft cloth or tissue. Use tepid water, try to wash the whole of one surface with one gentle stroke, wipe off the moisture with another drier cloth. If the dust is grimy or greasy as it is sometimes in cities, squeeze a few drops of detergent into the water, use this water and then rinse with untreated water.

Do not smear the leaves with oils or any substance other than water unless this be an insecticide. Pores can so easily be clogged with oils and once this happens the leaf cannot breathe nor work properly and it dies.

House plants sometimes become infested with insects as do garden plants. Quite often these will spread from one plant to the others. Some plants are notoriously dirty, cinerarias for instance. These seem to draw aphis to them. Inspect the undersides of their leaves every day.

Before you decide to buy insecticides and a syringe or atomiser with which to apply them, ask yourself if this is economic – sometimes the cure costs more than a new plant.

Do remember that insecticides are poisons and do not use the spray in the home. The only exceptions are fly-killers designed specifically for domestic use. Incidentally, these are often effective against a mild attack of aphis or greenfly. Otherwise take plants outdoors, out of the wind, spray them and allow them to become dry before you bring them back indoors. Read the labels and follow the directions carefully. Systemic insecticides can save some bother if you add a small dose to the water once a month because this will prevent serious infestations. Certainly use this method once you have sprayed a plant.

Most of the insect pests live by sucking the sap of the plants. This weakens the plant and it also can spread diseases. Systemic insecticides work through the system of the plant. If these are watered into the soil they can be taken up through the roots and then spread through the plant. Their action is not immediate, it might take two or three days before the poison reaches the pest.

If you are not squeamish, often the most effective means of ridding a plant of a pest is to squash it between thumb and finger.

Greenfly usually cluster first on young shoots of plants. You may be first aware of them either because the surface of a windowsill is sticky from their exudations or because spent insect bodies lie like dust under a plant. It is advisable to keep a magnifying glass handy and to inspect soft-leaved plants frequently. If you notice that a leaf has become distorted this also might be a sign of greenfly or some other aphis colony starting up. Instant action is often effective and the plant does not suffer a great deal.

Another reason why humidity is essential in the cultivation of happy house plants is that it deters the infestations of an unpleasant little mite known as red spider. Some house plant owners have never seen this little creature for it occurs only when the atmosphere is too dry. A badly affected plant will look rusty and this will be because of the thousands of tiny red mites, not really spiders, encased in webs which cover leaves and growing tips.

Apart from a plant not looking well, signs that red spider is present are brown even brittle leaves and many shed leaves. The mites usually collect first of all on the underside of the leaves and they are almost impossible to see with the naked eye. In certain lights it is easy to see the web but not always. The standard way of detecting this is to drop a little cigarette ash or to blow a little powder onto the underside of a leaf. If this clings you will know that the web is there.

Red spider is difficult to eliminate without total wetting with some proprietary insecticide. It might be best to discard the plant. If you do this be sure to clean wall surfaces, sills, flower pots or containers and to throw away soil or plunge materials used for the affected plant.

To prevent your plants from becoming infested make sure that humidity is provided. Spray with clean water wherever possible.

Mealy bug is another, milder, nuisance but it often attacks those plants which are difficult to treat, for instance, it will cluster down between the spines of a cactus. It is white or greyish and mealy, looking like a tiny piece of cotton wool which has become caught in the plant. This meal hides a nasty little sucking bug, a relation, I believe, of the cochineal bug. A spray of insecticide will not always reach the cracks and crevices in which these insects lurk and the best way to remove them is to take some methylated spirit and a matchstick and with lots of patience, scrape away at each little tuft.

Incidentally, I find that I can keep large spiny cacti fairly clean by passing the dusting brush of the vacuum cleaner over them each week. By the same method I suck out dead leaves caught up in the spines of euphorbias. Dead leaves often harbour mealy bugs. From time to time, gently shake climbing plants such as rhoicissus to release any leaves which may be caught up in the trails.

The most frequent disease seems to be mildew and the various kinds of mildews are caused by over-watering and sometimes a combination of too much water and too little heat. Some mildews affect the soils, some the leaf surfaces which become covered. Over-watering also causes wilts and root rots. Plants thus affected are really best discarded.

Fortunately, in spite of these awful descriptions house plant pests and diseases are relatively few and are not, or need not be, troublesome in most homes. The important thing is to keep watch on the plants and to keep them clean. Sponging and syringing leaves deter insects almost as much as more drastic measures do.

Increasing plants

There are some house plants which lose much of their appeal as they grow older, especially if they have to be confined to small pots. Some, like tradescantia become straggly and lose colour, plectranthus can grow too rampant and take over a shelf or some corner of a room, *Begonia rex* varieties can grow much too large for their pots and present an unattractive root portion in the centre of the plant, an aechmea after it has flowered may develop so many offsets or daughter plants round the main vase that it becomes top-heavy. All of these and others like them are best replaced by younger, neater and more vigorous specimens.

Many house plants can be very easily increased by some means or another. Stem cuttings can be taken from tradescantia and plectranthus and others and these will root in moist sand, in cuttings compost and even in plain water. Large begonia plants and many others can be divided into several smaller ones. The best of the mature begonia leaves can be used as leaf cuttings and will produce plants. Offsets from aechmea and many other plants can be detached from the parent plant and grown on individually. There are also other means of propagation, all simple, and within the scope of the most amateur gardener.

Those who hope to make many plant arrangements or pot-et-fleur arrangements will find that a stock of small plants will prove invaluable. Sometimes, you can use cuttings in the place of plants and these can be growing roots while they are part of an arrangement.

Cuttings are the easiest form of propagation. Often all you have to do is to nip off a growing shoot and simply push into another pot or into water, it is that easy. Cuttings vary considerably; they can be a shoot from the growing tip of a plant, a section of stem, a portion of root, a snip of a leaf or a full leaf.

The tips of some plants, such as tradescantia, plectranthus, rhoicissus, philodendron, impatiens and hedera are among the easiest of all. As a rule, the shoot is cut or nipped out about a quarter-inch below a leaf. The lower leaves or leaf are trimmed off, with scissors or a sharp knife to avoid peeling the stem, in case they lie in soil or water and so create a source of infection. The bare portion of stem is then inserted into whatever rooting medium is chosen. Usually one should aim to have at least one third the length of the cutting as a rooting portion. Hormone rooting powders can be used to accelerate the formation of roots. If you use these, follow the directions carefully.

The plants mentioned above can be rooted in plain water. Later when puddle-pots are being described, more names will be added to the list. Rooting compost can be bought but most cuttings root extremely well in a simple home-made mixture of half sand and half compost with a little extra sand as a top layer. Put a few stones or pebbles in the bottom of the pot first.

If you wish to save space you can plant several cuttings to a pot, inserted round near the rim in a ring. When they are rooted, tip out the root ball very gently and just as gently tease them apart and pot them separately.

Fill the pot, ram the compost down a little because cuttings root better in a firm medium, make a little hole to take the stem with a pencil or skewer. Take it to the required depth, remove and insert the trimmed stem. Push the dibber down at an angle at the side of the cutting so that it is firmed and the hole in which it is set filled at the same time. Give the pot a sharp tap to settle the soil and then water the cuttings.

Rooting mediums should be damp and they should not be allowed to dry out. To keep moisture in you can cover the cuttings in some way, with a jamjar or with a transparent plastic bag for instance. If possible let these covers stay on until the cuttings root. If excessive moisture forms inside the cover, remove it and wipe it dry. A plastic bag needs only to be turned inside out and the dry side is then inside. Should you see mildew forming on any of the leaves, pick them off and give the cuttings more ventilation by taking the cover off for a while each day.

If you strike cuttings in water you can easily see when the roots have formed. If the cuttings are in pots give them a gentle tug at any time after two or three weeks to see if they are anchored or not.

For those who enjoy indoor gardening, taking leaf cuttings can be rewarding in more ways than one. Actually, a great many house plants can be propagated this way but not in the casual manner I am about to describe. Most will need the warm, close, humid atmosphere of a special propagating frame, most practical to run in a greenhouse although it is possible to buy small electrically heated frames for use in a home.

Begonia rex leaves, or those of other types are extremely easy and the satisfying thing about these is that you can use them first in flower arrangements and then as cuttings. Insert the leaf with its entire stem under the water into a little vessel. This can be glass or opaque, it does not seem to matter. After some days roots will emerge from the stem base and then a little later a tiny cluster of miniature leaf buds will begin to develop at

Left
Fibrous-rooted begonias and some of the new tuberous-rooted varieties are easily raised from seed in a warm place. They are all very free-flowering and bloom for months on end.

Above
Chlorophytum elatum 'Variegatum'. The little plantlets produced at the tips of the arching flowering stems can be encouraged to make individual mature plants. These can each be directed into a pot of soil. When it has grown into this the plantlet can be detached from its parent plant. Plantlets can also be detached and rooted in water.

the junction of stem and leaf. Soon these grow into leaves and eventually you have a beautiful new young plant which often retains its mother leaf for a long time.

Peperomias, saintpaulias or African violets and gloxinias will root easily this way in the home. If you want to try others, take them and keep the cutting inside a glass storage jar or a transparent plastic bag in good light and in a warm place—even on a shelf over a radiator which is not a place I would usually recommend for plants. All of these can also be rooted in compost.

Another method of taking begonia cuttings is to divide the leaf in such a way that the leaf bud clusters are formed in several places on its surface. Lay the leaf face downwards on the table and cut through the thickest veins with a sharp knife making cuts of about a ½ inch from one side to the other. The cuts should be

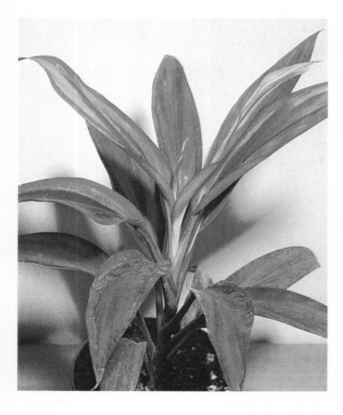

made at the point where the veins divide and on the side nearest the stem. Retain the stem—or at least about an inch of it.

Have ready a 50–50 mixture of peat and sand in a seed pan, flower pot saucer, special little propagating tray with plastic lid which you can buy for this purpose and for raising seeds or, and this I use, a shallow plastic food container with a transparent lid.

Holding the slashed leaf carefully in the palm of your hand, turn it the right way up. Gauge its length and make a hole for the short stem. Insert this as you lay the leaf flat. See that the leaf lies flat on the moist compost, weight it down here and there if necessary with a little more, just a pinch will do.

Plantlets should spring from the cut areas. Cover the box or pan with glass or transparent plastic. When the plantlets are well formed pot them up.

Some plants produce plantlets without being goaded into action this way. Some ferns form plantlets on fronds, some succulents on their leaves or like the bryophyllum in a delightful fringe round the margin of a leaf. These plantlets may be potted and will grow into large plants.

Other plants send out plantlets on the ends of runners or stolons. These remain on the parent plant until the little plantlet finds a home for itself and then the runner gradually rots away. In the home, we can direct these

stolons to drop their plantlets on a pot of soil ready waiting. Here the little plantlet will soon grow into the soil and all you have to do is to snip the umbilical cord. Chlorophytums send out a number of these stolons which add to the attractiveness of the plant. Often you will see the thick thong-like roots forming while they dangle in the air.

A similar method may be used for layering plants. In this case, one leads a good trail of any climber to a pot of soil, or even to a vessel of water. The stem is held down on the soil or in the water—a stone is usually the best means, just lay this over the stem so that it stays in place, and roots should grow from the part of stem which comes in contact with the rooting medium. Often roots grow quicker into soil if the skin of the stem is scraped away at this point.

Air-layering is a means of renewing, even tidying some plants. As varieties of *Ficus decora*, dieffenbachias and dracaenas grow older often the tuft of leaves is borne higher and higher on the tip of a stem which has become a trunk. As a rule the plants are not attractive so unless there is a special reason for keeping a tall plant it is best to air-layer the portion of plant at the top of the trunk.

At a point a few inches below the lowest leaf and with a sharp knife, mark a circle round the stem by cutting through the skin. Mark another circle about a ½ inch. lower down. It should now be possible to peel the skin away from this area. This should now be covered with some material into which roots, which should spring from the cut portion, will grow. Traditionally, moist sphagnum moss is used, a handful say about the size of a tennis ball, spread round the stem and then tied to it and finally covered with plastic to cut down loss by evaporation. Should you find it difficult to buy the moss, use a small cylinder of Oasis, cut down the centre. Soak this in water and then take the two halves and place them on each side of the stem. Press them against the stem and bind them in place and cover them the same way as you would cover the moss.

The piece of plastic—sheeting or even a clear bag will do—should be tied firmly both above and below the rooting medium. It is prudent to examine it after a few days to ensure that all is keeping moist.

Once you can see the roots through the plastic, the new plant can be severed from its parent stem. Rather than damage the new roots, pot the whole mass, i.e. moss or plastic and roots together.

You can see when a plant needs repotting often without knocking it from its pot. Turn it upside down and see if any roots are roaming through the drainage holes. With other plants, it is quite obvious that they are bursting their bonds and that not even a move into a larger pot will really benefit them. Primulas, some ferns, chlorophytums, aspidistras, begonias, impatiens are a few examples which come quickly to mind. Sometimes, and this is expecially the case with ferns and with large epiphyllums and aechmeas, the roots are so massed, that one can do no more than to cut the root mass into great chunks each with its own topknot of leaves. Others can be tipped out and sections simply teased out from the mass. Keep the new pots on the small side, just large enough to take the new root portion comfortably.

After dividing or repotting plants treat them a little tenderly. Water them in, as this settles the soil round their roots, but avoid giving them too much water, give them time to make new roots first. Spray them overhead so that their leaves are kept moist instead if this is practicable. Keep them in good light but out of the sun, even if they are sun lovers.

Left
Red Edge, *(D. marginata)* a delightful dracaena variety. These plants will grow for years, but as they age and lengthen their stems may become bare, something which can be masked when they are used in arrangements or in groups. Otherwise one can make 'new' plants of them by the technique of air layering.

Above right
A collection of various species and varieties of dracaenas will prove invaluable to the plant arranger. This lovely variegated form, tall and graceful, is *D. sanderiana.* It looks well grouped with wide-spreading plants.

Right
Begonia rex hybrids and *B. masoniana* may be raised from seed and they may also be increased by means of leaf cuttings. The latter is the best method to ensure more plants of one particular colour or leaf pattern.

Flower Arranging

Containers

Styles of arrangements for flowers in the home usually are based on the position or place in which the flowers are to stand, though of course, the flowers or plant materials which are used are themselves bound to have a great influence on the patterns into which they are arranged. Obviously, if one wants flowers, heavy stems and wayward leaves to remain in the position and place designated for them, one should employ some means of holding them secure. For this purpose we use stem holders. There are types to suit every purpose, as we shall see. Possibly the easiest to find and certainly the most adaptable and the cheapest is large mesh wire-netting.

One finds this indispensable not only as a stem holder for flowers, when it can be cut to fit any vase, but also for making cones to be studded with evergreens or flowers, for making pockets or nests to take fruits and gourds which are part of an arrangement but which

should not be in water, and as we have already learned, as a prop, wedge, heightener and support for plant arrangements. In fact, once he or she begins to use wire-netting, the flower arranger will find that it is often the answer to some decorative problem. For instance, certain shapes can be cut out from the netting and then decorated.

Small-mesh wire is not suitable because it is so stiff. Use large-mesh wire: 1½–2 inch mesh is best for flower arrangements because the wire is so pliable and will give as a stem passes through it, yet remain firm enough to hold the stems where you want them. If it is necessary to make an outsize arrangement in which the stems are really tall and tapering, cut a little more netting than usual and after filling the vase take several inches up above the rim of the vase. Place the tallest stem in position wrapping some of the netting, at the back of the container, round the base of its stem until it is secure. One can anchor great boughs of leaves and blossoms or tall stems of such subjects as pampas grass this way.

The usual method is to cut a piece of netting which measures twice the height of the container and a little more than its width. The netting is then crumpled up or bent U-shaped and inserted into the mouth of the container.

Some vases and other containers are so much easier to fill with flowers than others. Waisted vases or those that flute out at the rim and then become very narrow to the base are usually difficult to fill. It is certainly awkward to make some flowers in them fall prettily at a low angle. The way to deal with these is not to attempt to fill the vase with netting from the base to the rim, as is usual, instead, just measure the top width and set the netting in this area only.

This also is the method for using glass containers.

Previous pages
Double narcissi and tulips, hyacinths, leucocoryne and eucalyptus. When the arrangement is to be viewed from the front only, and not from all angles, the centre stem should be placed well back to allow room for many flowers in front of it.

Left
Carnations, roses, chrysanthemums and schizostylis (kaffir lilies) with mixed foliage and honesty. One vase stands inside another to make this deep arrangement. The top pedestal vase is filled with wire-netting and a ring of netting inside the lower vase encircles its foot.

Below left
Ornamental gourds, single chrysanthemums and elaeagnus foliage. Full of colour and exciting texture, a group of flowers, fruit and foliage makes an attractive decoration. Large fruits can be stood, like eggs in a cup, in jars which are easily hidden by the other components.

Below
'Apricot Silk' roses in glass. Because the neck of the glass is small most of these roses were arranged and tied in the hand. The two lower blooms were arranged separately. They wedge the bunch into position and hide the tie.

Right
This bright mixture of annuals mixed with a shoot from a pot coleus, is arranged in a bowl standing on a flat green pedestal dish. Low-lying flowers hide the water vessel.

Left
Pink peonies, delphiniums, spirea, scotch mist, sweet peas and pinks. The contrasting shapes of the full blooms and the spikey delphiniums give this arrangement fullness and definition.

Below
A copper jelly mould keeps water cool and sweet and brings a lively and natural air to the simple garden flowers.

Secure a smaller piece of wire-netting in the mouth of the glass only. If you have doubts about its stability, secure it in a few places, and on the outside of the glass where it will not become damp, with a few strips of adhesive tape. The flower stems can then pass down through the netting which will hold them as you wish, into the water, while the means of holding the stems is hidden. You can always arrange a few leaves or flowers below rim level so as to hide the least trace of the netting.

When using glass containers, put in a nugget or two of charcoal to keep the water clear. If, however, the water becomes cloudy as it does sometimes during very hot weather, do not disturb your arrangement but take it to the sink, part the stems a little at the back of the arrangement and let a cold tap run with force into the vessel. This will change the water and aerate it at the same time.

When you push the netting into any container, push the folded end in first and hold the netting so that the ends of the cut edge are uppermost. These can be used to advantage. You can crook them over a rim to hold the

netting firm – do this in three or four places if necessary. You can also use these little snag ends to embrace any very tall stems that need to be more restrained than others or which are heavy or inclined to turn about as some do, the forced guelder rose is an example.

If you want to make some stems hang down really low below rim level you can do this by hooking an end or two round them quite near rim level where the wire will not show. You can then exert gentle but firm pressure on the wire until the stems fall into the position you want. At other times these wire ends can be pushed through a stem, just as though they were pins. This will hold a stem just where you want it and yet do it no harm.

To return for a moment to glass containers. You can dispense with wire-netting altogether for these if you wish to arrange just one lovely branch or perhaps a group of flowers flowing at some special angle in the oriental manner.

Obviously whatever method you use, the important thing is that the holder should not show through the glass. It is possible, when you are using a narrow necked glass – or an opaque vase – to wedge one stem, or a very few stems, in place by pushing short, thick pieces of bare stem between the branch and the side of the container.

You can also use a lump of modelling clay the same way but if you do, remember that clay will stick only to perfectly dry surfaces so get it in place and the stem arranged before adding the water.

Simple and effective are the ancient Japanese 'kubari', either the forked or cross stick type. Kubari should always be cut from living twigs – cupressus is excellent for this purpose. First cut the twig so that it fits tightly in the mouth of the container. This may not necessarily be across the widest portion because the stem may look best flowing from some point near the rim, so test first. Split the wood and wedge it open with another small piece of the same twig so that it resembles a Y.

Cross twigs should first be measured in the same way and then simply fastened together at the centre with raffia or fine twine.

A very modern form of kubari is simply to cut a block of Oasis, about which I have more to say later, and wedge this in the mouth of the container.

Another effective way to hold one single stem, a branch of blossom for instance, is to bend but not break the base of the stem so that it makes a 'foot' at right angles to the main stem. This should fit snugly from one side of the base of the container to the other. This being

Previous pages
Poppy anemones. Buy or
pick *Anemone coronaria*
flowers before they open,
but not too young, or they
will not mature. To keep a
bowl going, add a few buds
each week and remove only
those flowers which drop their
petals.

Horse chestnut blossoms
can sometimes be heavy and a
little difficult to control. Pieces
of driftwood at the centre of
this arrangement hold the
stems in place and also form
part of the design.

Right
Chincherinchees and copper
beech. Pinholders are suitable
for arrangements in the
oriental style. Stems are
impaled on or across the
points. Leafy laterals pruned
from the main stem hide the
stem-holder and add to the
general effect of the arrangement.

Opposite page
Daffodils, aucuba and
chlorophytum leaves with a
giant sea-snail shell. Shells of
all kinds can be used in many
ways in flower arrangements.
This shell conceals the
pinholder. At the same time it
emphasises the curving lines
of the design. The deep green
leathery leaves of the aucuba
make very useful foliage
additions.

so the branch will stay upright and firmly in place.

An invaluable aid is the pinholder which holds stems impaled upon its points. Woody stems can be cut on a slant, or even split and then can be arranged at almost any angle. Pinholders come in all shapes and sizes. You can buy one, or a series of them, small enough and dainty enough for a wineglass. Actually, these little holders can be pressed against the side of a glass to hold one stem. Other pinholders are so large that they are heavy to lift but they are invaluable for holding a really heavy branch in place inside the vase.

Although they can be used inside a tall vessel, pin-holders are most useful for arrangements made in shallow containers. It is important that the pinholder does not move or slip about if the arrangement is moved. To prevent this happening simply make three or four peasized pills of modelling clay and press them under the *dry* holder. Do this lightly but firmly so that they adhere but are still rounded. Then turn the holder right way up and press it down on the container in the spot in which it is to stand. As the pills are flattened they provide a bond between the two which can later be easily removed.

If you would like to use a dish or a plate or some other object which is really too shallow to hold water, use a tin or small deeper supplementary container to hold the water and the pinholder. Place the clay pills under the water vessel as well as under the pinholder in this case.

Foamed plastic stem holders, such as Oasis, are great aids to the flower arranger. Made of foamed urea, their texture is soft, sponge-like and unresistant. They are available the world over.

Probably the most important thing about them is that you can so easily insert a stem into the surface where it will immediately hold firm. If the stem is very short, you need insert no more than 1 inch or even less. As you will appreciate, this is a great advantage because many lovely subjects, leaves in particular, are often very short stemmed. Should you wish, and you might if you were making Christmas decorations, you can even insert stems upside down and they will still stay in place.

Because the plastics absorb and hold water they can be used ex-container, that is to say, on a plate rather than inside a vessel. However, when it is used this way one should realise that the moisture will evaporate constantly and that the plastic will need re-soaking each day.

When used inside a container it is most convenient to put a square peg in a round hole, in other words, a rectangular block in a cylindrical vessel. This then leaves four spaces near the rim, and water can be poured into whichever one is most conveniently placed.

Obviously, it is a great advantage to have a variety of stem holders but where the arranger is working to a limited budget and in cases of emergency it is possible to devise many simple means of holding stems. Long ago, wet clay, straws bunched and pressed into a vase, and box snippets arranged to come just to rim level, were some of the means employed. The important thing is to ensure that the stem holder is so firmly wedged or anchored that it cannot move while the flowers are being arranged. As a rule, it is the first few stems that need most careful placement. Once these stand firm and as required, other stems which cross them below rim level inside the vase become locked and these then make a stem holder for those which follow.

For those who have no pinholders a large potato offers a good substitute on occasions. Its base should be sliced so that it holds firm. Woody stems can be cut on a slant and thrust into this. Larger holes can be made

with a peeler or an apple corer to take small and frail stemmed flowers which should be bunched beforehand. The potato is hidden with a cluster of stones which also anchor it.

Those new to flower arranging may find it interesting to note that hiding the stem holder in a low arrangement often anchors the flowers in such a way that they become welded to the container. And the way one decides to camouflage a stem holder can add to the interest of the arrangement as a whole. Often it is sufficient simply to arrange the largest leaves or flowers so low that although they are not actually in the water they are so near to the surface that they screen the holder. If the arrangement is in a vertical style to do this may not be right and then one resorts to the use of shells, stones, small gnarled pieces of driftwood, cork, bark, fungi—these can be dried and used again and again, actually, any natural material which has some beauty or interest to commend it. Pet shops stock certain items which make good accessories, coral, rocks, sea-fans.

Where it is essential that objects are kept out of water it is usually a simple matter to lay a piece of bark, plastic, cork or even a flat shell, across the container from one side to the other near the pinholder and to arrange them on this. Wire-netting can be used as a nest for the same purpose and in this case one can use leaves to hide it and place the other things on these.

Wire-netting can be cut and rolled to make a cone. Cut out a paper pattern first. The base can be pushed into the container and the flowers inserted all over the surface of the wire shape, through the netting, their stems down into the water. Alternatively, a cone can be stuffed with moss or damp foamed plastic. However, it is much simpler, especially if you are making several Christmas decorations, to buy the foamed plastic shapes ready-made for this purpose. These come in several sizes. They are also available in spherical form. These can be used to make floral bosses which can either be mounted on a stem like a little tree-trunk or suspended from a cord or ribbon.

Styles

Left
Many kinds of annuals fill this Victorian vase designed for two levels of flowers. The tall bugle-shaped container fits inside the bowl. One can improvise similar containers from everyday objects quite easily.

Right
Alliums and driftwood. Formal flowers fit naturally into formal patterns but there are many simple ways we can introduce a little informality without diminishing their effectiveness. Driftwood adds curves and hides the stem holder.

Below
Ranunculus in a Queen conch shell. There is really no limit to the type of containers you can use. So long as whatever you would like to use can hold water or some moisture-retentive material it will do. Shells and flowers go beautifully together.

One of the best pieces of advice I can give relating to flower arrangement is this: don't be tied in any way. Don't think that you have to have special vases, that you have to follow special rules, that you have to use only certain kinds of flowers, materials or colours. The way you arrange flowers should depend entirely on how you want to see them. However, I think that it needs stressing that flower arrangement proper means value for money and reward for time spent, which the mere placement of flowers can never be. Think in terms of buying a few beautiful flowers and spinning them out with foliage and other accessories. Collect a wide range of containers because these will help you ring the changes constantly and you can elect to use the same cheap flowers for weeks on end without ever becoming tired of them. Collect containers with the same liberal point of view as I suggested you should adopt when looking for those suitable for plant ar-

Left
If you have some fine leaves
often you need only a few
flowers to furnish a vase.
These are from the shrub
Rhododendron falconeri and
have velvety undersides which
harmonise with the orange
chrysanthemums 'Galaxy'.

Below left
Chrysanthemums, kale and
beech leaves and briza grass
in a wooden knifebox.
The attractive-looking fruit
can still be taken from this dish.
As it is replaced the colours
of the decoration may change
a little but not the character.

rangements. Apart from true flower vases—and so far as these are concerned do realise that some of these are difficult to use, especially the old fashioned types which need so many flowers to fill them attractively—you can use anything that holds water or which can be made to appear to do so.

If you make a collection of accessories for flower arrangements you will always have a source of decoration and of inspiration. These with your house plants will ensure that you can always rustle up a flower arrangement or a party decoration for some special occasion. Do remember that anything that grows can be used. Driftwood is particularly lovely for this purpose and it is worth while searching the beach to find one piece or more that is beautifully shaped, no

matter how small. If you find only small pieces they can be joined together quite effectively to make a piece which is shaped more to your liking. Such pieces can be given false stems or they can simply be laid or wedged in place.

Cone and certain seed heads, such as poppy, lotus, morning glories, proteas, camphor tree pods, all on sale at certain times of the year, will look like wooden flowers. You can arrange these with fresh materials as well as dried ones.

Most things lifted from the fruit bowl or the vegetable basket will look well arranged with flowers and leaves. Those crisp, vivid yellow coral-curly leaves from the forced rhubarb, large parsley leaves, especially if they are yellowing a little, frost-blue outer leaves of cabbage, even a whole little cabbage can play a part.

Many leaves will eke out a few flowers and give substance as well as beauty to an arrangement. Fern fronds and fallen leaves, picked up in the park perhaps, can be used fresh and then pressed and kept for some other occasion. If you have a vigorous leafy house plant, borrow a leaf or two from it. If possible, select those which you know you can treat as leaf cuttings after they have served their term in the decorations–the beautifully coloured leaves of *Begonia rex* are ideal for this purpose. Use trails of tradescantia, ivies, plectranthus and rhoicissus with all uniform flowers which could do with a little informality and root the cuttings afterwards.

A fruit bowl can become a flower arrangement with such little effort. Put a piece of well soaked Oasis in a waterproof plastic bag and hide it among the fruit. This will hold the flower and leaf stems. If necessary use two or more of these containers so that you can distribute the flowers well. Generally speaking, shiny blooms look better and cleaner with fruit than do those with soft petals. You can also use children's party balloons filled with water or tablet tubes to hold the flower stems as we do in pot-et-fleur arrangements.

The lovely texture of gladioli can take any of the brightest fruits, for none of these are likely to overpower the flowers themselves. This is a good way to use these flowers when they have past their best and the spike is no longer the complete beautiful thing it was. Snap off the tip on which there are still good florets and renew these by arranging them in a completely different manner. This is one example of what I mean about studied flower arrangement being value for money.

In its widest sense, flower arrangement falls roughly into two groups, formal–into which group fall the traditional arrangements, and informal. There are subdivisions of these groups. Generally speaking, the type of flowers often, but not always, guide us as to what style to use. As you will appreciate, uniform flowers, especially where only one kind is to be used in an arrangement, tend to fall into formal patterns. Indeed, so far as shop flowers are concerned, their perfect uniformity is often best exploited.

In our homes, we find that certain styles suit one place better than another. For example, on a table that stands in the centre of a room or round which people pass the flowers should be arranged so that they look good from any angle.

Decorations of this kind are called, for want of a better name, all-round arrangements. For a sideboard or for a decoration that has to be set against a wall it is necessary only to face the flowers so that they look out into the room. Actually this is a very economic style because you will not need so many flowers. These are known as faced arrangements.

On these two themes we can play many variations. Flowers for special little places about the home may not need to conform to any particular style any more than any other ornament in the house. These can be made truly pictorial or scenic. Alternatively, they can be sparse and oriental in style, expecially if some furnishing or other decoration nearby is in the same mood.

So far as traditional styles are concerned, think in terms of shapes, the shapes which you would get if you were to draw a line round the flowers' tips after they were arranged. This may sound complicated to a beginner but it is true to say that after doing only very few flower arrangements one can see how these shapes emerge, and by the same token, one can quickly appreciate which are likely to be the most suitable for one's own needs.

Let us take first a bowl of flowers arranged for a table

Previous page
Single chrysanthemums,
daffodils, holly, cotoneaster,
mistletoe and leucothoe.
Strong colour contrasts are
warm and welcoming in
winter and at Christmas also.
The forced daffodils should be
bought or picked in bud for a
longer vase life.

Top left
Mixed dahlias with parsley,
fennel heads and santolina
buttons. Short-stemmed
flowers look well massed in a
simple manner. Even so, each
one should be arranged
separately. Wire-netting holds
these blooms in such a way that
each one can be fully admired.

Above
Marigolds in a bowl raised on
a pedestal. Like some other
flowers, tulips and Iceland
poppies for example,
marigolds tend to go their
own way in an arrangement.
Vary stem lengths to give each
bloom space to display itself.

Left
Tulips, freesias, hyacinths and
mimosa in a work basket.
Wickerwork and flowers go
well together. Either line the
basket with foil or plastic or
install a water-tight container,
a tin for instance. Prop the
lid open before arranging the
flowers.

73

Narcissi in variety, tulips,
irises, hyacinths and guelder
roses (*Viburnum opulus*) red-
leaved maple and broom tips
in candlecups. When making a
pair of arrangements do them
together (arranging one stem
in each at a time) so as to make
them twins. Candlecup designs
like these can be used with
other flowers at any season of
the year. The all-round shape
of table-centre arrangements is
particularly important.

Below. See following page.

centre. Here you have the choice of several shapes.
Which one you select will depend upon the size of the
table and the occasion. If no one is to sit at the table the
arrangement could be high, wide and handsome. But,
if you were arranging the flowers for a dinner table it
would be best and more polite, to keep them low. A
small table needs only a small decoration at its centre
while a very long table could have flowers along most of
its length – or perhaps a line of three or five bowls.

The pattern most often used is a half-sphere or globe
which is resting in its container which may itself be
another half-sphere but this is not essential. This pattern
can also be made in a rectangular trough.

As a variation, the side flowers may be elongated so
that their arrangement is in the shape of an egg sliced
through the centre. In a different manner, the tallest
stem may be much longer than the side stems and the
intermediate stems adjusted accordingly and then you
have a cone.

No matter which of these three basic patterns you
select, there is one rule to remember for all-rounders
if you want to learn to do them quickly and effectively.
The centre stem should always be plumb in the middle
of the container and it should be the only stem that is
upright. This is where you will find the little wire-
netting cut end hooks so useful. They help to make a
bent stem upright. Hook one or two round the stem
where it stands up from the netting and gently press on

the wire until the flower head or the tip of the stem is dead centre. After this, every other stem which is arranged should lean away from this central stem even if the angle is only very slight.

The side stems, which should be arranged next, should be at a really wide angle to the centre stem. While the centre stem defines the height of the finished arrangement, the side stems will define its width, and all the other stems should be kept within these dimensions.

For formal faced arrangements, imagine that we slice an all-rounder down the centre so that it becomes a semi-circle, a half oval or a triangle in outline. The centre stem is still the only one that is perpendicular but now it is moved to take up a central position but, this time, as far back against the rim of the container as possible. This is so as to leave plenty of room for all the flowers that are to be placed before it.

Flower arrangements need to have depth and this is an easy way to achieve this effect. Given so much space in front of this centre stem you will be able to arrange the blooms at different levels and to recess some, thus adding to the general interest and avoiding a flat over-formal surface.

Once again all the stems which follow this centre stem placed well back against the rim should lean away from it either to the left or the right, as the case may be. Stems should never be seen to cross each other above rim level. Instead, try to make every stem appear as though it had sprung from a source at the base of this centre stem.

If you can, let the decoration taper at the edges. If you have twelve or ten flowers almost identical and little else to arrange with them, you will find this impossible – one reason why I suggest that it is helpful to collect some accessories. Where flowers seem too much alike, introduce contrast of shape, slender stems such as grass, gladioli leaves, pencil rushes, small-leaved ivy trails, or the spike like flowers of a delphinium. However, even if you have only a bunch of flowers all exactly alike you can still create a flowing or growing effect.

The all-round arrangements just described were for bowls and fairly low containers but there are occasions when this type of arrangement has to be made in a tall container. In such cases one simply follows the same procedure.

To avoid a squat appearance or one in which the container appears to dominate the arrangement, try to make the central stem at least one and a half times the height of the container when measured from the point where it rises from the rim. If by doing this – and because you have no choice of container – you find that the arrangement would be too tall for a table centre, adjust the proportions by making the tallest stem reach the required height and arrange the side stems and all the lowest materials so that they flow over the rim and down the sides and so conceal the true height of the container.

Many arrangements in low shallow vessels have the flavour of the orient about them even if they do not precisely conform to the rules of the ancient and traditional Japanese flower arrangements. These were very strict but even in today's styles they can be helpful. You may not be sufficiently attracted to true Japanese styles to want to copy them but you may find that by studying the principles which underline them you could benefit greatly for they are based on observation and sound common sense.

The basic shape is an irregular triangle and quite often there are only three flowers or stems in an arrangement. These are known as *shushi*. If additonal stems are used these are known as *jushi* and when they are arranged they are always placed within the pattern,

Previous pages left
'Super Star' roses match scarlet sweet peas. Styles of flower arrangements have to be based on the role of the arrangement itself. Those which are to stand on a dining table should be low so as not to be in the way. However, you will still need some long stems to obtain the length of this arrangement – remember to check that all stems are in water all the time.

Previous pages right
Delphiniums, roses, anthemis, and gypsophila in copper. When round flowers are massed, use spicate shapes to taper the edges of the arrangement. As well as delphiniums, grasses, rushes, leaves and sprays of foliage, blossom and berries can be used.

Above left
Lilies and driftwood. The method one uses to camouflage a stemholder can add to the interest of the arrangement as a whole. Three small pieces of driftwood, carefully placed, here look like one wonderfully contorted piece.

Left
Gladioli and desert spoons. Really the bases of faded agave stems, desert spoons are just one example of the many natural, long-lasting plant materials that one can buy or collect to use in flower arrangements.

Right
The fleur-de-lys outline of irises is so lovely that one should give each flower room to display itself. Their uniformity is softened by the curving driftwood which also helps to hold the shell in place.

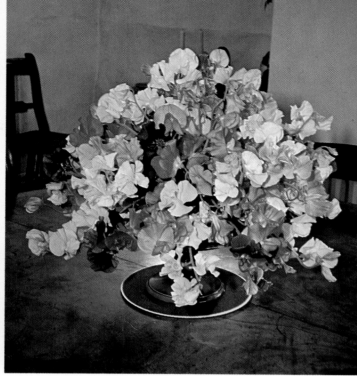

outline or dimensions set by the *shushi*.

These three main stems are said to represent heaven, earth and man, *shin*, *soe* and *hikae*. The important stem is *shin* and this one should always be the tallest. It should also be curved and its tip should always be over its base. No matter how curving or undulating this stem might be it is controlled by this rule. The next in importance is *soe* and this second stem is placed to the side of the main stem, and indeed, as it rises from the surface of the water or from the rim of a tall container, it runs so close to *shin* that the two look like one stem. After a little space *soe* should move away to follow

its own way but it must never reach more than two-thirds the height of *shin*. *Hikae* is the lowly stem, as befits its name. It should always occupy a low position in an arrangement. It should flow forward but never downward.

When *jushi* are used, these are always added last, and as a rule just three or five are considered sufficient.

From this basic traditional style many others have evolved and even break-away groups have evolved their own styles also and so it is not possible to speak of one modern Japanese style. Apart from the rigid rules, which not everyone appreciates, the value of these

Left
We do not slavishly have to follow Japanese rules to create a similar delicate and tranquil mood in our own arrangements. Here the soft lines of winter flowering peach, carefully pruned, frame a few early Christmas roses or hellebores, their white petals contrasted against the deep green leaves.

Top right
Sweet peas and petunias, both of which are quite long lasting if they are gathered young enough. The first should have only the lower flower on a stem open wide. Petunia buds should be well coloured.

Far right
Sweet peas in a Wedgwood comport. Cut or buy sweet peas with at least one bud still to open. Arrange them in shallow water or in foamed plastic. Petals must be kept dry or the flowers will rot, so shake off rain or dew before bringing them indoors.

Right
Roman hyacinths, Christmas roses (*Helleborus niger*) and double tulips. With only 1 inch or so of their stem ends in water, these hyacinths are stretched to their limit. This way just a handful of flowers will make a good-sized decoration. Water should be topped up daily.

styles lies in the fact that they teach one to use very few flowers. This is a contrast to western traditional flower arrangement in which masses of flowers were and are used, but it is important to stress that you do not have to follow the rules of Japanese flower arrangements to make attractive decorations in which only few blooms are used.

When we use few flowers we concentrate on the beauty of line. For those who have to buy all their flowers line arrangements are both fun and quick to assemble. For instance, for a quick and attractive arrangement, take five irises, daffodils or any uniform flower. Arrange the flowers in your hand so that each bloom stands a little above the other. Cut the stem ends level. Stand them on a pinholder in a low dish. Move each one slightly away from its fellow to give it room to grow. At the foot of the stems and to hide the holder, arrange leaves, shells, fruit, seed pods, coral, whatever you have. To make a simple variation on this theme arrange the stems on the holder so that the flowers form a curve, a crescent or an S. This curving line need not be upright. There may be occasions when you think that it would look better flowing to left or right.

Arrangements in which a branch, bare, leafy, berried, blossomed or lichen-covered, or even driftwood, is featured with a few flowers can look very lovely in spite of the fact that they are also very economical. Choose a branch for its own sake, the more twisted and curved the better. Failing this, prune a fairly straightforward branch so that it assumes more the character you want.

For such arrangements, set the pinholder in the dish either in the centre or to one side – often the latter is more effective. Set the branch on the pinholder and then begin to work on it. Pull at the stem gently until the tip is over the centre of the base of the container and only when you get this to your satisfaction begin to introduce other materials. As we have already seen, the manner in which you hide the pinholder can contribute to the effectiveness and beauty of the whole arrangement.

If you buy foliage to eke out your flowers you will find that most branches are too heavy, too dense or the wrong shape. These need breaking down and dividing and even then you are likely to find that some foliage needs removing. Often the leaves you remove can be used elsewhere.

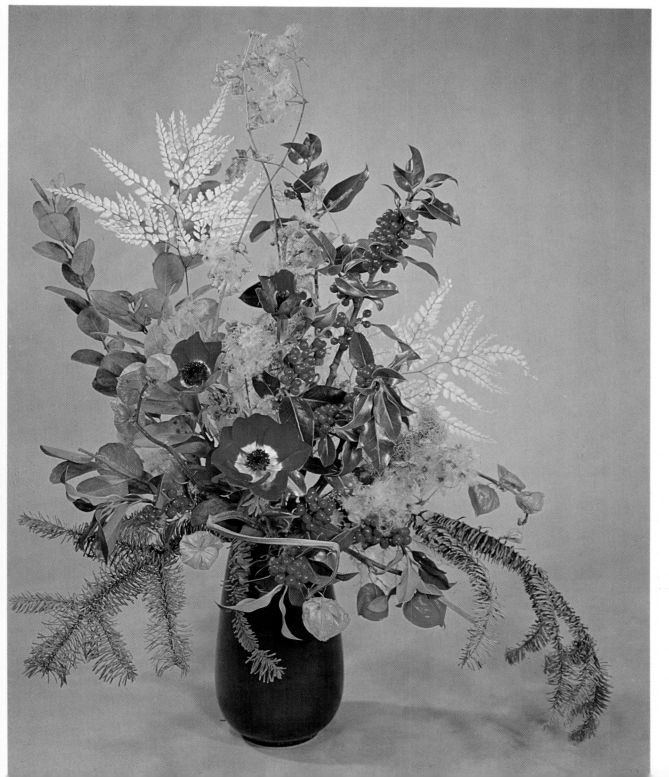

Opposite page
Iceland poppies (*Papaver nudicaule*) and briza grasses. Some flowers, including all poppies, are best cut in bud, just before they are ready to open. They will then last many days in water. Poppies should always have their stem ends singed before they are arranged to prevent loss of latex.

Left
Poppy anemones, physalis (Chinese lanterns), adiantum fern, holly, clematis seed, blue spruce and autumn coloured foliage. There are only three fresh flowers in this arrangement. The added value of an arrangement such as this is that you can keep it going for weeks if you change the water regularly and remove and replace the flowers as they fade.

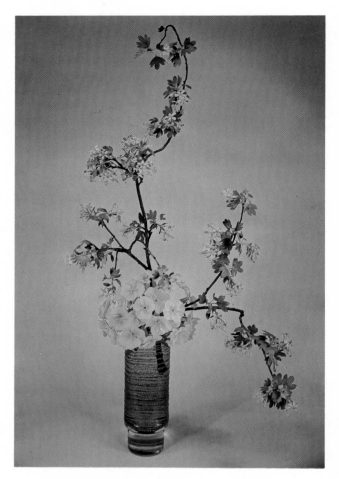

Often one bunch of flowers can be broken up to make several arrangements which contain three, four or five flowers. The effect of the arrangement will depend on the placement of the blooms and the accessories. These do not necessarily have to be arranged in low containers. For instance, three tall chrysanthemums can be arranged, one above another in a tall vase with a flurry of some other materials at rim level, perhaps some berried bunches, leaf clusters, or even a bunch of some other flowers, say a posy of scarlet anemones, depending upon the colours used.

Three flowers of medium length can be given height by using branches, pencil rushes, gladioli leaves placed behind them. If these are all arranged in a tall vase the desired effect will be even greater.

One way to save both time and flowers is to make a permanent framework of leaves before which you can arrange a few flowers helped out with fruits, foliage or whatever you can find. As the fresh blooms fade, these can be easily replaced, even with a different kind of flower altogether. Some foliage is so long-lasting that such an arrangement can stay in position for weeks. In spring you can adopt the same principle but with different materials, using burgeoning blossom and spring flowers with perhaps, a flowering house plant or two.

There are some flowers that flag or wilt badly, examples are pyrethrums, hot-house roses, forced tulips, yet once we can get them to take water they perk up and last well. Almost always the cause of flagging is an airlock which forms in the stem and this affects some flowers more than others. Usually the woodiest or the most fibrous stems, such as stocks, are the most temperamental.

Never begin arranging flowers as soon as you get them home except all narcissi. These have tough, hollow stems and even if the flowers are a little dry and flagged they quickly drink and perk up.

When flowers have been out of water for some time, often really hot water treatment is best. Otherwise,

stand them in luke-warm water – baby-bath heat, for at least an hour, longer if possible. Those which are really badly flagging and any which have been stood in luke-warm water but which have obviously not taken any, should be stood in 2–3 inches of boiling water. Let them remain there until the water has cooled and then arrange them in unboiled but luke-warm water. There are exceptions, never stand bulb or corm flowers such as narcissi, tulips, lilies or gladioli in hot water. The stems will just collapse. Always stand paeonies, delphiniums, chrysanthemums, scabious, pyrethrums and most annuals in hot water to begin with.

Frail, delicate-looking flowers such as annual gypsophila and saponaria and fern fronds and small-leaved soft subjects such as maple are best drawn through the water, shaken gently to remove surplus moisture and then arranged. Very young and immature foliage often needs immersing for a few minutes, but if you buy this it should already be hardened or conditioned.

Stems that bleed, that is, exude a white sticky sap or latex, can be sealed best and most quickly by pushing the cut stem into sand, but of course this is not always handy. It is possible also to stem bleeding by pushing a little dry Oasis on to the wound. You must treat the stem again if you cut it shorter when arranging. Plants of this nature include the poinsettia.

It should not be necessary to change the water each day for flower arrangements. What is important is that there should be no vegetation under the water except the stem. Leaves, except those of tough evergreens, quickly decompose and turn the water smelly. Even the evergreens will rot in time if they are left under water long enough. Always strip the leaves from any portion of stem which is to go under water. A word of warning, do not overdo this or you may find that there is a very bare zone above the rim of the vase. Top up with fresh water each day.

Take care though that no leaf touches the water while its tip is over or on the rim of the container because this might create a siphon and you will then find a pool of water on some precious piece of furniture and an empty vase.

Some flowers last best in shallow water. If you have had gladioli that snap their stems after arrangement they are probably getting too much water. Just 2 or 3 inches is sufficient for them and most other bulb or corm flowers. Forced tulips however, need a deep drink before arrangement. Sweet peas last best in bowls in shallow water than in deep vases although if these are all you have they can hold a little rather than a lot of water.

A lump of sugar or a teaspoonful to a pint of water will help to feed flowers and keep them looking lovely for a little longer than usual. You can also use a saltspoonful of honey to a pint of water or even a glucose tablet. Most of the proprietary life-lengtheners have sugar in them and are well worth using if you are not budgeting very carefully. An aspirin tablet or a copper coin does not help the flowers to live longer because they do not check bacterial activity. Flowers live no longer in metal containers for the same reason. For evergreens and branches you hope to force into early blossom, use a few drops of liquid plant food or a half of a plant food tablet in the water to keep them going. Do not stand glass vessels in a window or in sunlight or the water will soon be so active that the flowers it holds will die.

Although it helps some flowers and plants to be lightly sprayed with clean water from an atomiser, others will simply discolour if water falls on their petals. Fortunately, these are not numerous, most prone are all kinds of violas and sweet peas.

Above
Yellow flowering currant branches and polyanthus. This is a good way of using short stemmed flowers which also need two thirds of their stems in water if they are going to last well. The natural line of the branches dictates the shape of the arrangement.

Right
Rhododendron, crab apple, lilac and irises. If blossom is cut in bud it will continue to thrive in the vase. It will last longer if the arrangement is not moved. Cut the foliage from the lilac to prevent the blossom from flagging.

Dried flowers

It is possible to preserve certain foliage so that it keeps its shape and general character. Usually the colours change; deep green laurel, for instance, becomes a warm chestnut brown, but this is never a disadvantage. There are as many nuances in tone and hues in these broken colours as there are in the primary green.

The method of preservation is as follows: mix one part glycerine with two parts boiling water. Pour 2 or 3 inches of the solution into a narrow jar or tin or some other vessel and stand the stem ends in it. Let them remain until you can see that the solution has travelled right through all the tiny veins in the leaves. At this point, the texture usually changes becoming silkier and softer. If the branches are allowed to remain in the solution too long they will sweat and the sticky exudation may fall on to the furniture. It is a simple matter to decide when the leaves are sufficiently charged with the solution.

Most flower shops sell certain imported foliage during the winter months and so long as these take water easily they can be preserved and stored for future use and used time and time again. To make sure that these can be preserved, as soon as possible split the stem ends upwards for about 2 inches (this applies to all branches deciduous and evergreen) and stand them in 2–3 inches of hot water, at boiling point is best. Let the branches remain in this for several hours, overnight if possible. After this time you will be able to see which branches are not taking water, the leaves curl and look dry. These will not take the glycerine solution although it may be possible to use them dried. If you have patience to press the individual leaves with a warm iron most foliage can be salvaged and used many times, examples are grevillea, oak, beech. Others can be opened as flat as possible and laid between newspaper and then under a heavy object, mattress or cushion for example.

Any blue gum or eucalyptus is, as its name suggests, pleasantly grey-blue. There are roughly speaking two kinds which are marketed: the species and varieties with round penny-sized leaves and the long kind whose leaves are bent sickle-wise. Sometimes the latter kind may be bought complete with lovely silver-grey buds and coral-like tassel flowers. The buds will dry. These eucalyptus stems can be given just forty eight hours in the solution and this period seems long enough to fix both the form of the leaf and the colour. It is also possible to take eucalyptus from the preserving solution at different intervals and so have the leaves in various stages of hue. The longer these stay in, the darker the leaves become. Most subjects take more than four weeks.

Most often people preserve those leaves which are turning colour in the autumn. To do this, one should always cut or buy the branches long before the leaves begin to fall.

Once the leaves are preserved they will last for years. They can be used entirely in dried flower and perpetuelle arrangements or they can be used from time to time with fresh flowers. Indeed, merely by preserving a few leaves you can have sufficient foliage to be able to furnish a vase with just a few flowers the year round and yet make good-sized decorations. If you preserve a little of several kinds you can frequently ring the changes. Store them away in some dry place in boxes or in plastic bags. If the stems have been stood in water, wipe them and make sure that they are dry before putting them in store.

As we have seen, a variety of any plant material makes flower arrangement easier and I would suggest that you try experimenting with various types of foliage to see which can be kept. If you buy gladioli or irises which have good entire healthy leaves, you might like to treat these. They turn a pleasant tan and they offer a contrast of shape.

You may also find that some of the leaves from house plants can be preserved–worth while doing if a plant, a cissus for instance, has grown too large.

Incidentally, certain leaves and infloresences, faded though they may be, are worth saving. Bromeliad blooms such as aechmea and vriesia look well in a large perpetuelle arrangement. Aspidistra leaves will last for years. You can curve these–and the gladioli

Left
Eucalyptus, stachys (lamb's tongues), rhodanthe and helichrysum with purple sea lavender (limonium or statice). Eucalyptus keeps its colour when dried. The large straw-daisies, helichrysum, are threaded on wire stems. Little rhodanthe flowers are bunched and then can be lengthened, tied to straws or mounted on wires.

Below
Grasses, honesty (lunaria), limonium and acroclinium. Lightweight vases should be one third filled with sand or shingle. The stemholder can be arranged on this. These stems are held in dry Oasis.

and iris leaves—by coiling them, tying them in place lightly with thread and then leaving them to soak overnight. They should then be dried thoroughly, after which they may be unloosened and pulled out to assume the necessary curves. Other leaves, such as shadow leaves, the name given to skeletonised magnolia and ficus leaves, and all those sold as magnolia can be given curves by coiling them round a candle or the handle of a wooden spoon.

Whether or not you wish to use only true flowers is a matter of personal taste. There are many manufactured flowers today. These are made from real plant parts but are not true flowers. They are attractive in their own way but generally speaking they are stiff in appearance so it is necessary to use plenty of informal material with them.

Look out for the bright orange Chinese lanterns or physalis, on sale in late autumn. During the summer buy small spikes of delphiniums and full spikes of annual larkspur and hang these upside down to dry in some warm, dry, dark place, an airing cupboard for instance. Buy grasses. Few of these on sale are in their natural state, they are either bleached or dyed, but if the dyed grass is of the colour most dominant in the arrangement you are planning it will not look too artificial. Slim pencil rushes keep for years and are a good buy. Most of these retain a bare portion of an inch or even much more above the flower portion. They look more attractive when this is cut away.

These attractive brown stems suit so many winter decorations and they look so right with tawny chrysanthemums, dried flowers of all kinds, fruits, berries and autumn and winter foliage.

One winter decoration which is very quick to do and most effective consists of five or seven pencil rushes,

the stems cut so that the 'flowers' are slightly fanned These are impaled on the back portion of a pinholder Shadow leaves or any large leaves, fresh, preserved of pressed, are then arranged so that they too taper from one down to a fan on the left or right.

The tallest should reach to about halfway up the stem of the tallest pencil rush. Those that need to be tall are given false stems, usually the portion cut from the shortest pencil rushes. As a focal point you can use a large cone, or a gourd, surrounded by a star of flower grouping of smaller leaves. You can use fronds of stipa grass to soften the outline.

False stems are easily applied and if you want to make the greatest use of many of the very decorative short-stemmed subjects they are essential. Use straws even drinking straws if you have no true tough grasses thin twigs such as privet, lilac or even woody flower stems. Pipe cleaners are almost as useful as florist wires. These can be twisted round the short petiole or stem of any leaf. Where other types of false stem are used, fasten the true stem to its mount with adhesive tape. Pine cones need false stems. Usually one has to encircle the cone near the base, pulling the wire or cleaner right down so that it is wedged in the base of the scales. The ends of the wire stem are then taken down under the cone and twisted round each other Cones make lovely wooden flowers and look well with brown preserved foliage.

Various stem holders may be employed to hold the materials. Since dried materials are usually very light in weight they need anchoring in some way. Dry Oasis is one of the best holders because one can insert even the frailest stem without breaking it. This can also be used in shallow containers in place of a pinholder Oasis-Fix, a putty like adhesive will hold it firmly.

Home Decoration

Placing plants

If you go out specially to buy a house plant, it is more than likely that you already know exactly where you want to place it. If someone gives you a plant, the case is altered because then you have to find a place in your home for it. Light, the source of light, the quantity of light, the warmth of light, the aspect of light are all important to all plants.

Some of those which do not do well in our homes need more than we can give them in the average house. Those which are adaptable and easy to grow find that conditions in a home are not so very different from those of their natural surroundings, even though the means of providing those conditions may differ considerably.

Many of our popular leafy house plants grow naturally in the shade of the jungle forests. They grow in daylight but in the kind of daylight which is filtered down through a ceiling layer of leaves. Surprisingly,

perhaps, this jungle light has much the same degree of intensity as does the light inside our homes. This explains why so many jungle plants make good house plants.

On the other hand, the popular flowering plants, mostly, have originated in sunny open climates and, as we have already seen, the more flowers a plant has the more light it needs when it grows indoors. Sometimes it is impossible to give it the amount of daylight it requires but there are methods of adjusting this, as we shall see.

The same conditions are required by any plant which has some colour other than green. All variegated foliage, leaves of two or more different colours, needs good light. However direct sunlight can cause more harm than good. The pretty scindapsus for instance, placed in strong sunlight will soon develop brown edges to its marbled leaves.

One might think that a windowsill is the natural place for any plant, especially after learning that a plant must have light, but one must realise that even windowsills receive different degrees or amounts of light according to what aspect they face. Fortunately, north, south, east or west-facing, we can find plants to suit any windowsill. Simply bear in mind that the sun pouring in early morning from the east will have nothing like the burning intensity of the sun shining in a south facing window midday or one which faces west on a late, hot, summer afternoon. North-facing windows tend to be both shady and cool and are ideal for many, indeed one might even say most plants, so long as the room itself is warm as well.

You can actually witness the influence of light upon growth. If you leave a plant undisturbed in a window it will, as you may know, gradually turn all its parts to

Previous pages
Columnea x banksii is a lovely and accommodating house plant which is too seldom seen. Its pretty trailing habit, with its masses of flowers, make it highly decorative. It likes lots of light but not direct sunlight.

Left
You can have plants in flower at all times of the year, even when snow falls thick outdoors! Here, *Euphorbia splendens* towers above an echeveria in bloom, bowls of mixed cactus and succulents and 'Peach Blossom' double early tulips. On the right is a yellow-flowering *Euphorbia splendens lutea*.

Below left
Facing a window in a corridor, *Hedera canariensis* has its roots in comparative shade, *Aechmea fasciata*, tradescantia, croton (codiaeum), anthurium, a poinsettia (*Euphorbia pulcherrima*) which has flowered and the rarely seen *Scindapsus pictus* 'Argyraeus'.

Below
Ficus pandurata. The large, tough green leaves indicate that this fig should be grown in much the same way as the rubber plant. It needs slightly warmer conditions and care with watering.

face the light, and leaves and flowers will show only their undersurfaces when seen from the room. If you want a plant to grow evenly, it is important to turn the plant a little each day, so that eventually all parts receive the same amount of direct light.

We can exploit this tendency. It is possible to grow a great many leafy plants on walls which are opposite to a window or a glass door and these plants will become extremely decorative because they will gradually turn their leaves to face the window. This means that for those people in the room itself, the plants show their best faces.

Fortunately, there are many plants which will grow well this way, all the green-leaved climbers and creepers, for instance. Remember, the greener, thicker, tougher the leaf, the further back from the light the plant can be grown. Bromeliads will also flourish here and if you are so inclined your wall can be decorated by a tree on which a collection of the smaller types of these plants can be fixed. Driftwood, or stripped clean tree branch, or pieces of cork bark made to look like a tree portion, can be used as an anchorage. Alternatively, one can use a good looking plastic mesh and fix the plants on this.

In some situations it is possible to grow variegated plants this way, for instance, in a corridor or hallway where the opposite wall is not really very far from the window. Variegated ivies will roam prettily, especially the large-leaved *Hedera canariensis*. *Scindapsus aureus* and its varieties can be used for smaller effects. This pretty little scrambler looks well planted at the foot of the large-leaved ivy. Mix it with the dark-leaved plectranthus which has purple undersides to its leaves and will provide contrast.

Another position in which plants look attractive and where, at the same time, they are in a more suitable position, is at right angles to a window. Here, according to the size and style of a room, one can place a shelf, a table, a large container, a group of plants stood on the floor, or a trough.

When they are grouped this way you can often use one or two plants to shield the rest from intense light. Place those which revel in it, a *Euphorbia splendens* or an outsize cactus for example, near the glass and graduate the rest so that those which prefer the shade are furthest away from it.

If you plan to use a trough under or in a window, bear a few points in mind before you install it. Remember that the plants will face outwards in time, if the trough is on the windowsill itself, or even if it is placed immediately below it, unless you are prepared to turn the trough every few days. It is possible to choose plants which look very attractive with the light shining through them. Some of the ornamental begonias, and there are enough of these to give you variety, would be suitable for this purpose and if you have a really warm room in winter, *Iresine* 'brilliantissima' could be gorgeous. If you grow climbers in the trough, and these can look so attractive trained around, or in the case of an unsightly view, on the window, remember that these do best if their roots are not in full light. Either screen the base of the climbers with bushy plants or stand the container out of the light.

Those who know their subject talk of light levels, and the levels of light influence plants in different ways. Light has colour and although a detailed study of this is not the subject of this book, we should say that the colour of light affects a plant so much that it will become drawn or elongated or tight and compact according to the kind of light under which it is grown. Daylight does not offer us many problems in this respect.

How long light shines is another factor in growth, we call it the duration of light. This affects the develop-

ment of flowers so much that light duration is the basis of many horticultural methods used to produce flowers out of their natural season, such as poinsettias and all-year-round chrysanthemums. It affects us in the home in a simple way – we can use artificial light to prolong daylight and thus grow a greater range of plants.

Not all of us want to place plants in a window. In many homes there is not a suitable area in windows anyway and we have to place the plants in other areas about the home. Many of us feel that a corner, a dim hall or some other place could be enlivened if only some plants could be induced to grow there. But what really is the point of doing this if the plants cannot properly be seen? If they are lit some way, you ensure not only that the plants can be seen but also that they will be happier and will look more decorative simply because they will receive more light.

You will find that artificial light, even a reading lamp placed nearby and left switched on for four or five hours, greatly improves a plant's performance. If you have one which appears to have remained static for months, try putting a lamp near it and watch the new

Opposite top left
Many plants grow best if they are arranged at right angles to a window, with those which tolerate the strongest light placed nearest the glass. Here are ananas or pineapple, dracaena, chlorophytum, sansevieria, *Begonia masoniana* or the Iron Cross begonia, with the blue flowers of browallia nearby, *Begonia rex* hybrid, cyclamen, crotons (codiaeum) scindapsus and vriesia.

Opposite top right
Monsteras and bromeliads add colour and life to a kitchen which has enough space to accommodate them. The humidity and warmth of a kitchen (and even more of a bathroom) often make these rooms good situations for plants.

Opposite below
These plants are growing in a hall which has only one small window. However, white walls and a mirror placed strategically behind the plants reflect what little light there is and so help to increase light intensity.

This page
The monstera is botanically *Philodendron sellou* and like many others of this family, makes a handsome and distinctive climber. It is most effective where it can be given space to display its attractive leaves.

rate of growth. Plants in living rooms often do so much better than plants which grow in rooms which are used only occasionally.

You can improve the light intensity in a room and at the same time direct a little more light on to a plant by a few simple means. Plants grow better where there are light painted walls than they do against dark backgrounds. A strategically placed mirror, or better still a wall covered by a mirror, will reflect light from a window or from some other source, on to a plant.

From these few observations, you will see that it is always a good plan to site your plants with an eye on the room's lighting as well as according to their own light requirements. Generally speaking, our reading lamps give off white light and although plants really have a preference for blue with red light (not to be confused with the colour of light bulbs) when these two colours are properly balanced, the ordinary home light is efficient enough for us to leave the complexities of light colours to the commercial grower. I use only ordinary lights in my own home and house plants grow happily in every room. If you have an understanding of lighting systems, you could possibly work plant wonders.

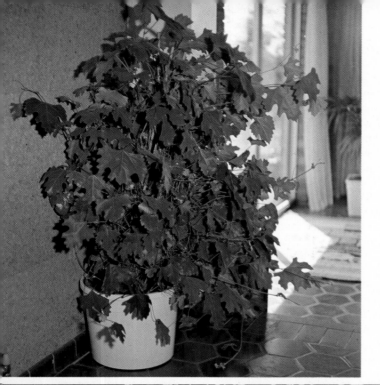

Various forms of lighting can be used from 100 watt bulbs placed no further from plants than 4 feet and no nearer than 2, this is because the bulb generates heat and if placed too close the plants will become scorched; to strip and even spot lights. Fluorescent lighting provides cool light and thus eliminates the danger of scorching. Some plants, such as saintpaulias can be grown entirely under the influence of such lighting where it is not possible to provide daylight for them.

In another section we deal with plants in bottles or jungle jars, the term which covers all glass containers. Here I should mention that these gardens should never be stood in full sun, yet the plants must receive enough light or they will damp off and die. It is possible to provide them with both heat and light by converting the jungle jar into a lamp. You can buy fitments to fix into the neck of most of these glass containers and these will hold both the light bulb and lamp shade. The important thing here is that by such means the light is directed down on to the plants. As it is more ornamental than useful, the light is subdued and so cannot harm the plants.

Left
Rhoicissus capensis. Strong-growing climbers, especially those belonging to the grape-vine family, should be given plenty of room and encouraged to climb. Given support they will soon cover a wall. *R. capensis* is a strong growing vine with woody stems and leathery leaves. It has attractive red fruit after flowering.

Below and right
The leaves of plants naturally turn towards the most important source of light, a tendency which can often be used for decorative effect. The darker green and the tougher the leaf, the further away from the direct source of daylight will a plant grow. Many climbers can be trained along a wall opposite a window.

Using the same principle, plants can be housed in a cupboard with glass doors, or in an alcove. The important thing is that the plants should never be grouped or grown with a light bulb close under them directing its dry warmth up to the plant's roots.

One of the kindest things plants can do is to bring life to a hearth no longer or seldom used for a real fire. The fireplace, so long as it is draught-proof, is an ideal place to grow plants. Here they can be watered and sprayed without harm. Many of the hearth and fireside accessories make attractive containers. One can, for example, pull out the ash pan under a fireplace, line it with strong plastic or a few layers of cooking foil and plant or plunge in this. Scuttles, coal boxes and hods, log baskets and large preserving pans and others can be filled with a variety of plants. If lighting can be installed the variety of plants can be greatly extended. However, even without this, there are plenty of plants which will thrive at this distance from windowlight, aspidistras, palms, syngoniums, philodendrons, spathiphyllums, bromeliads, sansevierias, for example.

Use plants to their greatest decorative advantage. If you are only just beginning to furnish a home, let them fill in the gaps meanwhile, you can always move them along when you have something more permanent. Let them act as screens, frames, furnishings. Let them mask a dreary scene, take attention away from an ugly or shabby corner. Use them to make a room look taller, wider, homelier and more welcoming.

Containers for them can be as varied as you wish, although it might be more pleasing if you search out only those which go with your general decorating theme. Make sure that the containers suit their setting and that they are deep enough to take the plants and then set about making the plants look as though they really were at home.

Certainly encourage climbers to climb and to do this you will find that strong thread and drawing pins are as good guides as anything else, but remember also that many climbers will also trail prettily. These look best if they can hang down from a pedestal, shelf or torchère. Some, such as ivies, look well cascading from the base of some very formal plants such as a *Ficus elastica* or sansevieria.

Most strong-growing climbers such as cissus, rhoicissus, ivy and several philodendron varieties can be trained to climb up in the corner of two walls and along the top of the wall in one direction or another, or, if it suits you, right round the room. To support the plants, you can stand a cane from the container to the ceiling or you can tie one end of a thread to the short cane to which the plant is already attached. Take this up vertically and pin it securely to the ceiling. Take more thread along the top of the wall near the ceiling or in whatever direction or angle you prefer. The thread is inconspicuous and really most effective. Obviously, it needs to be strong, and nylon fishing line is ideal because this will hold even weighty stems.

If you are going to use plants at high levels do remember that warm air currents rise and that the plants could suffer because of this. Those with lush growing tips such as philodendrons are more likely to suffer than say, rhoicissus. To prevent these from drying out, and so long as this does no damage to surroundings, spray the growing tips, and the rest of the plant if possible, with a little water, rain water preferably, from time to time. Use an atomiser and water at room temperature.

Grouping plants together successfully is not difficult and is never repetitive. Here, near a window framed by a rhoicissus are double tulips, a giant hippeastrum (so easy to grow), a striped vriesia in flower, crotons in a copper preserving pan and a stag horn fern or platycerium. The balance and shape of the group changes all the time as plants grow, flower and fade. It is fun to experiment and put together contrasting leaf shapes, textures and colours. Bulbs often look spectacular against plants grown principally for their foliage.

Right
Varieties of *Tradescantia fluminensis:* 'Quicksilver', top right 'Variegata', bottom left *Zebrina purpusii* is centre left and *Z. pendula* right; all these plants need good light if they are to be well coloured. Tip cuttings can be taken easily from both plants and they should be repotted each year.

Below
Perennials like the shrimp plant, African violets and anthurium to the left will continually produce flowers. Cyclamen, cinerarias and primulas among others can be grown from seed and timed to bloom in winter.

Plant arrangements and dish gardens

In spite of the multitude of flowers on sale in our markets it is a fact that there are more kinds of plants, in other words, a greater variety, than there are cut flowers. Since this is so and since the plants themselves are such good value for money, why not use more of them in the same way that flowers are used, in arrangements about the house? True, a flower arrangement has its own special aura and beauty and can never be entirely replaced, but a plant arrangement will last

Far left
Pot grown eranthus or winter aconites, double tulips and yellow hyacinths arranged with chlorophytum in a shallow trug basket. Driftwood and moss hide and support the bulbs which are planted in potting compost.

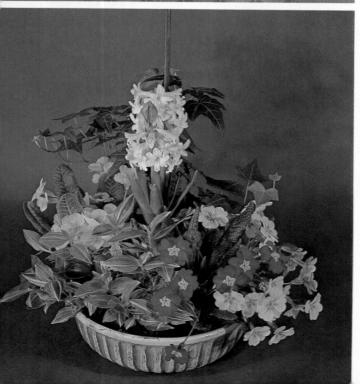

much longer and changes shape as the plants grow.

It is one of the best ways of decorating centrally-heated homes for we can provide humidity for plants and so minimise the possibilities of adverse effects from the heat, but we cannot prevent fresh flowers from maturing and fading quickly.

We can make arrangements from foliage plants alone or they can be mixed with shorter-lived bulbous and flowering plants. They can also be grouped with cut flowers which can be refreshed from time to time as they fade and it is worth observing that flowers arranged with growing plants and sharing in the more humid micro-climate around them, do last a little longer than those which are grouped on their own.

Plant arrangements vary considerably, after all; even a trough planted with a number of different kinds or several of one sort, is a plant arrangement. However, we can make more imaginative and decorative arrangements than this.

One can use plants which are left in their pots and these can be plunged into various mediums, as we have already learned, or they can be simply packed round and wedged into position with damp moss or with one of the water-retentive foamed plastics, such as Oasis, which are used in flower arrangement. Alternatively, plants can be knocked from their pots and transplanted. Generally, we refer to the first method as arranging plants and to the second as making a dish garden but, as we shall see, the dividing line is not always absolutely clear cut. Sometimes we used both methods in one container.

We can also make arrangements with cuttings of all kinds, stem, leaf, offsets and stolons, in such a way that these will root in the water, although you can also arrange rooted cuttings, and they will go on growing so long as we remember to feed them with a weak soluble plant food from time to time. This is a simple and effective way of growing little plants and a good way of using any tips you may think it prudent to nip out from a vigorous mature plant. It is also an ideal way for a new indoor gardener to learn a little about propagating plants and growing generally.

The cuttings or plants are held in position by small stones or pebbles. Shingle is excellent for this purpose and is usually easy to find. Any water-tight container will do for this type of dish garden, known as a puddle pot, so long as it is deep enough to hold a good layer of pebbles. All manner of bowls and little bygones such as sauce boats, tureens, lidless teapots and large shells—so long as the water does not spill from these when you move the arrangement—and certain types of flower vases are vessels which can be used.

Generally speaking, the shallower the container the more securely you should anchor the plants.

If pebbles picked up from the seashore are to be used these should be well soaked and the water changed several times to remove the salt. Whenever pebbles and water are used to grow plants always lace them well with nuggets of charcoal to keep the water sweet.

Stem cuttings which will root in water include tradescantia, zebrina and any of this family; small leaved philodendron—unless you are to make a large puddle pot in which case some of the other larger-leaved kinds could be used; ivies, the small-leaved kinds look particularly attractive; syngonium and many other aeroids, plectranthus, peperomia, coleus, impatiens, rhoicissus, cissus, vitis, and even some outdoor annuals such as nasturtiums.

Chlorophytum offsets, especially if you select those whose roots are already well grown will soon begin to grow.

You can use small rooted plants, almost any kind if you do not mind them living but briefly. For more

Previous page left
If hyacinths are grown singly in pots, they can be arranged together or with other plant cuttings when in bud. Here there is a cutting of ivy roots in the same potting soil. Moss and driftwood cover the bulbs themselves and the soil round them.

Previous page below
Aeroids are diverse in form and habit yet they blend well one with another. In the bowl, still in their pots, are variegated scindapsus and flowering anthuriums. Behind stand monstera and syngonium.

Left
Wickerwork and other non-waterproof containers can be lined with strong sheet plastic or cooking foil to prevent the water from plants escaping and spoiling furniture. Here, still in their pots, are arranged a variegated hibiscus, *Maranta leuconeura* 'Erythrophylla', tradescantia and fittonia–a collection of plants all with striking foliage which complement each other.

Centre left
A piece of driftwood and moss help to mask the pots in which these plants are still growing. The arum-like flower is the bloom of a spathiphyllum. Sansevieria and *Phoenix dactylifera*, the date palm, tower above *Hedera canariensis* on the left and *H. helix* on the right with a tufted chlorophytum at the centre.

Below left
Planted for a Mothering Sunday present this little bowl contains coloured primroses, a hyacinth, ivy and tradescantia. The two latter will go on growing in the bowl for a long time. The flowering plants should be removed when they have faded and be replaced with fresh colour.

Right
A copper preserving pan comfortably holds pots of citrus, pilea 'Moon valley', *Calathea makoyana*, and the tiny-leaved *Ficus pumila*. Moist peat fills the spaces between the pots and generates some humidity, which is necessary for the pilea and the calathea in particular. All these plants should be shaded from direct sunlight.

settled existence choose cyperus and carex, both swamp lovers. Wash the soil from roots before you arrange plants.

Although plants grown this way should be fed, they will never make such large specimens as they would if well grown in soil, but they do live for a long time. They are very dainty, with smaller leaves, more delicate trails and for this reason these little gardens give one the opportunity of using a greater variety of containers for plants than might be the case. And it follows, that this being so, one can use plant arrangements in more varied ways. For instance, such an arrangement in the right container can look delightful on a dressing table or on a desk. Puddle pots make good table centres, especially if you arrange some lovely glowing colour at the centre. This could be cuttings of coleus, some snippets or leaves from some bright-leaved begonia, or even, as a temporary measure, a little posy of fresh flowers. You could also grow or transplant some of the smaller bulb plants such as the pretty little Roman hyacinths which flower before Christmas, or crocus or any type of bulb which will grow well this way. Your choice will have to depend upon size because many of the forced bulbs are tall.

Many attractive flowers can be grown from bulbs planted in pebbles and water. This method seems to suit some narcissi particularly well but crocuses, hyacinths and, nowadays, even one variety of tulips, can be grown this way also. To make sure not only that you buy the correct types and varieties but also that you are kept up to date on new kinds, study a bulb merchant's catalogue and make your selection accordingly.

Any variety of narcissi recommended for indoor growing is almost certain to grow well in pebbles. The bunch-flowered or polyanthus varieties are said to do even better when grown this way than when grown in bulb fibre or soil indoors. Certainly I grow them successfully year after year.

To plant the bulbs, take a fairly deep bowl, the deeper the roots can go, the more securely will the bulbs be anchored, place a few nuggets of charcoal on the floor of the bowl and fill it to within 2 inches of the brim with the pebbles. Sit the bulbs on these, as close as you like so long as they do not touch. The noses of the bulbs should be well above the rim so adjust the level of the pebbles before you add water should this be necessary.

Right
Old fashioned double daffodils grow well in pots of soil. Tall 'Harvest Gold' are growing in fibre. Double tulips, scillas, grape hyacinths and hyacinths will all flower at the same time and can be complemented by cineraria.

Below
Like many other spring-flowering bulbs, crocuses can be grown in water anchored by stones or pebbles. A little charcoal keeps the water sweet. Crocuses are best kept in a cold place until the flower buds show when they can be brought into a warm room.

Above
Treat some plants as though they were flowers and make some beautiful decorations. Here the old ironstone tureen holds a matching cyclamen, a *Begonia masoniana* and cascading over the rim a *Plectranthus oertendahlii* with purple-backed leaves.

Left
Planted in good potting compost and growing happily together are *Ficus benjamina*, *Hedera canariensis*, with a vivid poinsettia and striking striped aphelandra before them, *Peperomia hederifolia* and *P. glabella* 'Variegata' with variegated leaves scrambling over the rim.

Right
A wonderful variety of textures, colours and forms can be brought together in a plant arrangement. Here at the centre is a croton or codiaeum, behind it are sansevieria, *Pittosporum undulatum*, and *Hedera canariensis*. Tradescantia and vriesia are in front with *Hypocyrta glabra* on the left and aphelandra on the right.

More pebbles should now be arranged round and between the bulbs so that these are upright and well supported. Pour in water, clean rainwater if possible, so that its level is just under the surface of the pebbles. Place the bowls in a cool dark place until the roots are growing well. This is usually between five and eight weeks according to the type of bulb.

Bulb fibre is also an easy medium in which to grow bulbs and it suits many kinds including all of those which can be grown in pebbles. It should be used moist but not sodden and, once again, the noses of the bulbs should be above the surface after planting.

The critical time for spring-flowering bulbs grown indoors is immediately after planting. The essential factor is that the bowls or other containers should be stored in a cold, dark place until the roots are well formed and the shoots are actually growing out from the bulbs. They can then be brought indoors. This is best done in stages, first into a cool place for a few days, and then into a warmer one and so on. If the bulbs are not treated this way you might find that the flowers are stunted, malformed or unattractive in some other way.

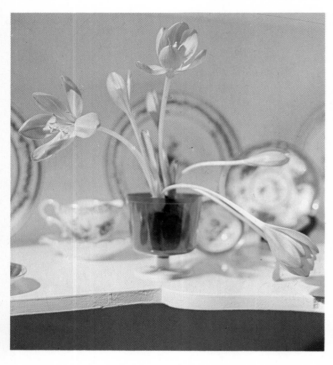

After trying many methods of cool, dark, storage including traditional plunging of bowls out of doors, I have found that the simplest and most effective way is to wrap each bowl inside a black plastic bag and to stand this in the coldest place you have—not the freezer though. I keep mine on the north wall of the garage, indoors. I have kept them outdoors on north-facing windowsills and roof areas, on a cold landing of an outer staircase to a flat and in a cellar. Any of these places will do.

As I said earlier, bring the bowls into the warmth and light gradually and once you have them in a window, give them a quarter turn each day to keep them growing evenly.

Whether you force your own bulbs or buy them ready grown be sure to water them, but once they are in bloom give them very little or they will mature too quickly. Always water the soil around the bulbs and try not to pour water over the bulbs themselves. When you spray your other plants to freshen them, give bulb flowers a little shower as well. They will keep fresher longer.

It is not really a good plan to grow mixtures of bulbs, although it is pleasant to make arrangements of different kinds if these are mature together. As you would expect, bulbs can be easily fitted into all manner of plant arrangements, in or ex-pot. You can plan a bulb and plant arrangement well ahead if when you plant a bowl with bulbs in fibre you also plant one or more empty flower pots. When the bulbs are brought into the warm room, you can then remove the empty pot and replace it with a full one. This could be another type of bulb flower, for instance, crocuses with narcissi, or it could be a flowering plant, such as a cyclamen, or a leafy plant or two.

If the bulbs are growing in pebbles and water you can introduce any of the puddle pot cuttings. If you do not mind being extravagant, you can wash the roots of an anthurium and plant it among the pebbles because this plant will grow happily this way. It will thrive also alone in a hyacinth glass.

To prevent them from becoming spoiled, metal and wooden containers can be lined. Quite often a strong waterproof plastic bag will do—you can cut it or roll it down so that it fits the container and is inconspicuous. Cooking foil offers extra lining and so far as wooden containers are used indoors, if these are precious and not simply plant troughs, it is wise to use foil and plastic.

Incidentally, speaking of plastic bags, those black sleeves, sold as substitutes for flower pots, are often much easier to fit into containers than the rigid pots. If you are building up a stock of small plants for plant arrangements you might care to bear this in mind.

Sometimes a shallow container can be given extra height and so made suitable for a plant with a deep root ball by lining it with foil or plastic and raising it at the back. This subterfuge will be hidden by plants arranged in the foreground. You can also retain the soil by using pieces of cork bark, driftwood and flat shells inside the rim.

The pleasant thing about using plants with flowers, or about grouping flowering plants, is that many containers one might pass over if one were looking for a container for a single plant, or for a collection of green plants, prove to be perfect when flowers are introduced. Old wash basins, which are often highly patterned, are ideal especially in cottage interiors. They are deep enough at the centre to take a large pot with a tall plant yet shallow enough at the edges to take the small pots in which hedera (ivy), tradescantia, plectranthus and other scramblers are often grown and wide enough to allow one to build up a really good collection.

As I said earlier, the dividing line between a plant arrangement and a dish garden is not always clear cut, and using a wash basin could offer an example of this, for I would suggest that where the area near the rim is too shallow to take a small pot comfortably, it might be more convenient and effective to add soil at this point and to plant the scramblers. Alternately, strike cuttings of them and let them root here to be moved later when the arrangement is dismantled.

The types of containers which can be used are legion. They include large soup tureens, coal scuttles, preserving pans, log baskets, urns, pitchers, to mention only a few.

Obviously, one has to be guided by size for a large container filled with potted plants can be very heavy and difficult to move around. One can lessen weight by filling a deep container to the required depth with foamed plastic. The pots can be pressed into this and they will be held at whatever angle is required. A further advantage is that the plastic stays nicely moist, or will do so if it is watered from time to time, and thus will generate a pleasant humid area immediately around the plant. Just one word of warning, plants find this substance so agreeable that after a time they grow down into it, so if you think it time the plants were repotted, examine the pot bottoms from time to time.

Left
Colchicum autumnale (often wrongly known as the autumn crocus). Flowers will grow from this bulb without the assistance of soil or water and in a very short time. Simply stand the bulb in some vessel or saucer to anchor it. After flowering, plant the bulb in the garden where it will produce its leaves in spring and flower again the following autumn.

Right
Plants need not be transplanted when they are arranged. All of these—dracaena, coccoloba, anthurium, cryptanthus and scindapsus are in their individual pots, some of which are raised and hidden by the Coccoloba.

Ingredients for a puddle pot are simple: gravel, water and a few nuggets of charcoal to keep it sweet, an attractive container and a selection of house plant cuttings. Arrange the cuttings as you would a vase, with trailers over the rim of the container and an interesting focal point in the centre – a coleus shoot in this case. Strip the stem ends of leaves before anchoring them in place with some of the shingle or whatever other stones are used. Finally, top up with water and feed the plants from time to time.

From my own point of view I find tall or pedestal flower vases to be some of the best containers for displaying house plants. Grouped in these, the plants are lifted well above the level of whatever surface on which the arrangement is to stand. They give elegance to arrangements, especially when trailing plants can be allowed to cascade down over the edge for some inches. There is another point to be borne in mind. When you have to move the arrangement you can do so easily and without disturbing the plants in any way, simply by holding a portion of the pedestal.

While bulb bowls are not in use they can hold plant arrangements and, of course, not all of these need be large, often three or four small plants look quite attractive especially if the container is a little out of the ordinary. If you have a choice, bear in mind that a container with sides that slope so that its mouth is much wider than its base gives you a good area of soil surface on which the plants can display themselves. If the container is deep, 4 inches at least, there is room for some roots near the base to reach down to the bottom and for others to be spread out nearer the surface.

As the containers you will use have no drainage hole it is necessary instead to install a layer of what is termed drainage material on the floor of the vessel. This provides essential air spaces into which water will be rapidly sucked when the plants are watered. One of the best drainage layers and certainly one of the most simple to provide today is made of small nuggets of charcoal. At one time broken flower pot crocks were recommended but these are becoming rarer and rarer. Stones and shingle may also be used but they tend to make the bowl very heavy.

The first rule for a successful dish garden is to provide good soil. Although the plants will retain their pot soil or root balls, more soil will be needed to pack round them. Do not use soil dug up from the garden or countryside for this may contain harmful pests and fungi. Buy a bag of good potting compost. This is on sale in garden shops and chain stores. Buy small amounts unless you are making many dish gardens because the soil mixture deteriorates during storage.

Before deciding which container you are going to use, examine your plants. The depth at which they should be planted is determined by their crowns, the part of the plant at the junction of root and top. The crown should never be further above or below the new soil level than it was originally.

In the finished arrangement, the soil surface does not have to be level, indeed it is usually better if it is not so. Raise it either in the centre or to one side. A raised soil area gives a plant greater depth for its roots. If you have plants from varied sizes of pots you can plant those from the largest pots in the raised soil area. At this point also, place those plants which like to be well drained, sansevierias, peperomias, succulents and bromeliads.

Having decided what plants you intend to grow together, water them and let them drain well before you begin, that is, unless they have been very recently watered. Knock them from their pots one at a time as you proceed so that their roots are not exposed to the air any longer than is necessary. Before you begin it is a good plan to arrange the plants on the table in roughly the pattern you intend to follow. You will then be able to see what placement is really practical and where the tallest or shortest plants ought to go.

Spread a layer of soil over the drainage layer. Do not make this too deep or you may have difficulty in accomodating the plants. As you arrange their roots on the soil, determine whether and where the soil needs raising. Try to disturb the roots as little as possible.

Below
Sedum sieboldii. A plant that will withstand quite cool conditions and because of its semi-succulent nature can be left for several weeks without water. It dies down in winter.

Most plants should stand upright but if you want some to trail over the rim of the container or to lean away from the centre, tilt them and slip some soil under them to wedge them in place. At the end, see that all the roots are covered with soil. Press this down firmly so that the plant is as solidly anchored as if it has been growing this way always. However, guard against panning the surface, that is making it so hard that water cannot pass through it easily. If it flows off, the surface is too hard.

Make sure that you have left room for watering. The soil level should be at least a ½ inch below the rim, even if it rises in the centre.

Finally, water the plants carefully, preferably by spraying the leaves and the soil surface. It is important that the soil is not made sodden. Stand the arrangement in its place so long as this is not in a very sunny spot.

If after some time, during which the plants have grown well and spread over the surface, you find it difficult to water the bowl it may be best to lower the whole arrangement gently into a sink filled with water or into some other larger vessel. Hold it there until the bubbles stop rising to the surface, then allow the surplus water to drain away. Cacti often need this method of watering but remember not to do this more than once a month in winter.

It is not wise to mix cacti with other kinds of house plants. Fortunately, these make charming arrangements when grown together and you can find sufficient variety among them to make contrasts of shapes and textures. Some succulents go well with them, especially those with bloom on their leaves or those which flower well such as rocheas and crassulas. Sansevierias can be grown with cacti.

Some succulents can be mixed with the majority of the other house plants you are likely to use in arrangements. Again, try rochea and crassulas, *Sedum sieboldii* 'Medio-variegatum', is a prettily variegated plant. Although it dies down in winter it is well worth collecting.

Whether you make a plant arrangement or a dish garden, aim for contrasts. Most groups look their prettiest with a plant or two scrambling over the edge of the container. In the central zones plant rosettes or distinctive broad-leaved plants such as the beautifully marked *Begonia Rex* varieties, calathea, maranta, pilea and some bromeliads. For height and grace there are palms, sansevieria, *Fatsia elegantissima*, ivies trained vertically, dracaenas especially the prettily coloured *Dracaena marginata* and the green and white striped *D. sanderiana*. There are many more.

Below
Most kinds of cacti and succulents will grow well and last for years in a shallow dish garden. In this one a small juniper has been added as a temporary contrast, since it will have to be removed and transplanted later.

Bottle gardens

Bottle gardens or jungle jars as they are sometimes called are extremely decorative and even appealing but apart from these qualitites they can also play a useful role. In them it is possible to grow many plants which cannot be expected to do so well outside the glass walls, in rooms where the atmosphere is dry and the temperature sometimes fluctuates. Of course, it is possible also to grow similar plants within the glass as are on the outside, but if a bottle garden offers you the choice of adding to your collection of house plants, why not take it and have a new arrangement to place as well?

Some of the more choosy plants you can expect to grow—and can buy—are species of selaginella which are mossy and fern-like and carpeting; *Nertera depressa*, another carpeting plant with tiny leaves and little orange berries, many kinds of the tender ferns such as the wiry-stemmed maidenhairs, miniature tender palms, crotons, fittonia, calathea, maranta, peperomia, pellaea, pilea and pellionia.

Some of these you will recognise as being good room plants under certain conditions and the important thing about using these in bottle gardens is that they are fairly slow growing. They also provide colour and texture contrast. It is possible to fill a bottle with just one type of plant, say a colony of bromeliads or ferns, but usually they look more attractive when the plants are mixed.

Unless you know your plants well, do not be led into thinking that if a plant is small and has small leaves it is bound to be suitable for this type of garden. Helxine now known botanically as *Soleirolia soleirolii*, sometimes called baby's tears, has the tiniest leaves yet it would soon take over the entire bottle. The same applies to the creeping ficus, to tradescantia and zebrina. Of course, if you find that a plant is growing too rapidly you can always take it out and pot it in the usual manner and grow it elsewhere. If you have a bottle garden for several years, this becomes necessary.

Jungle jars have become so popular that today special glass containers are being produced for this purpose. Unlike the old-fashioned glass carboys these are made with necks large enough to allow an arm to reach down inside. Another and easy-to-fill jungle jar is an outsize brandy balloon type glass. Storage jars and even wine and cider jars and bottles can be used, so long as it is possible to plant them.

The glass is usually clear but it can be tinted, light brown, light blue and green. The important thing is that it shall be clean and kept clean.

If the neck of the glass is large enough for you to insert your hand, planting will offer few problems but when you are filling a jar which has a narrow neck you should be both careful and patient.

First group the plants in the way you hope to see them in the jar. I suggest that you slope the soil, so keep this in mind, remembering that this will heighten any plant you set at the top of the slope.

If you cannot insert your hand you will need to improvise a tool or two so that you can make a hole for the plant, guide the plant into the hole, cover it and firm the soil round the plant afterwards. Often one thick stick will do the lot but more often it is helpful to lash a kitchen spoon to a cane to use to dig out holes. An old-fashioned wooden cotton reel on the end of a cane will make a neat little rammer with which you will be able to pat the soil round the plants. These should always be set firmly in the soil otherwise their roots will not be able to absorb nourishment and they may sicken and die.

As with all containers, troughs, large bowls, dish gardens, a drainage layer is essential. The safest thing to throw or pour in is charcoal which is so light in weight that it cannot crack the glass. If you use small pebbles such as pea gravel, do not pour this straight into the jar on to the glass base, but first pour in a thin layer of peat to cushion the impact of the stones.

To fill a carboy, make a funnel or cylindrical chute of strong paper or card. Insert one end of this into the neck of the jar. First pour in the peat, then the gravel and lastly the soil.

This drainage layer needs to be quite deep, 2 inches

Top
Planting a bottle garden. Make sure that the inside of the glass is sparkling clean before you begin work. Strew a few nuggets of charcoal on the floor of the container before adding some sand for drainage.

Slope the soil slightly. This is easily done if you put the lowest plant in first near the front, cover its roots with soil and put the next plant in position. Be sure to secure the roots of each plant and at the end gently ram the surface to firm it.

The little cryptanthus has been tied to a mossy branch and arranged out of the soil. The selaginella and tiny fern will carpet the soil, while the shrubby variegated euonymus and carex rush will provide contrast of shape and colour. Selaginella has small, scale-like leaves like a tiny fern and the species that are low growing and creeping are ideally suited to the cool humidity of a bottle garden.

or so for a large carboy and proportionately less for smaller jars.

Soil composts should not be too rich or the plants will grow too fast. The best medium is John Innes Potting Compost No. 2. The amount of soil you use will depend upon the size of the container; you should be able to see more glass and plants than soil but it is the depth of the plants' roots which should guide you. These must be properly planted.

To get the soil in the right condition so far as moisture is concerned, calculate how much you need, take about one third of this amount and spread this out on newspaper to dry. Spray the other two thirds until it is just moist, uniformly so, and when you take a handful and squeeze it gently it should just cling together.

This dampened compost should go in first. The dry compost follows to form a top dry layer which should help to seal in the moisture.

As with dish gardens, water the plants beforehand and allow them to drain thoroughly. Knock them from their pots in turn. If the aperture of the glass is very small it may be necessary to shake off any loose soil from the roots so that the plant can be slipped in easily. The leafy portion is no problem because this naturally contracts as it is pushed root first through the opening. To make sure of this, hold the plant by the tips of its leaves, or if it is tall, gather its branches or leaves up near its centre stem, so that this top portion is made really slim. Make a hole in the soil, tilt the jar and aim for the hole. This actually, is easier than it sounds. Direct the plant into the hole with the stick or with the spoon. Make the hole for the next plant directing the soil round the roots of the first plant. Ram the soil down before tilting the jar for the second time. Continue this way until all the plants are in position.

Inevitably, some soil particles will dirty the inside of the jar. It is not wise to spray these off with water, which seems the natural thing to do because the soil will be made too moist. A feather duster fixed to a strong piece of wire, which can be bent as required, is the easiest way to clean the glass. If the plants' leaves have soil on them, lash a fine paint brush to a cane and clean them.

If the soil is properly moist the plants should settle in and you should not need to water it for some weeks. If the balance is right you should see a little condensation or dew on the interior each morning. However, if this seems excessive—so much that there are several runnels and large drops on the glass, there is too much moisture in the soil and it would be prudent to remove the moisture from the glass to prevent it running back into the soil. Lash a tissue to the end of a wire or the bow of a coat-hanger to do this. When the time comes that you see no condensation, this is an indication that the soil needs watering. To do this, gently spray the interior glass. This will help to clean it at the same time. Do not feed the soil or the plants will grow too well.

Combining plants and flowers

Once you enjoy arranging plants you will not find it a great step to use cut flowers with them nor to add to these two all the accessories and lovely natural materials which are associated with flower arrangements.

You might begin, as I did, from a purely practical need. If a bowl of mixed plants looks a little spent and needs brightening, what could be easier or more instantly effective than to push some kind of water vessel into the soil, among the plants and hidden by them, and then to fill it with a few fresh flowers? You need so few and yet the result is often quite remarkable.

From such a simple beginning, you will find that pot-et-fleur, as such arrangements are called, offers you a most interesting and exciting way of decorating your home. In the first place, you will never be at a loss for basic colours because the plants will provide these. All you have to do is to find the few flowers that are required.

As you would expect, those which grow on plants akin to some of our house plants always look good in pot-et-fleur. These are such flowers as anthuriums, arums, cyclamen, which though they may seem a little expensive at times should last well. Orchids, also extremely long lasting, look delightful with house plants as do any of the smooth-stemmed bulb flowers; in spring, narcissi which include daffodils, freesias, tulips, and later in the year, gladioli, lilies, nerines, *Amaryllis Madonna* (the outdoor plant) and the late-flowering schizostylis.

Many shrubs' blossom looks good, especially in winter or early spring; magnolias, azaleas and rhododendrons, taken from their usual environment and set among exotic house plants have an extremely rich and wonderful effect.

Generally speaking leafy subjects look too fussy and if these are to be used it is usually best to remove most of their own foliage so that the house plants take the limelight. Examples are roses, paeonies, dahlias.

In the same way, soft petalled flowers may not show up as well as you had hoped, anemones and chrysanthemums, for instance.

You can often use a few flowers to emphasise a certain feature of a plant's foliage, colour for instance. Often the underside of a leaf may be vividly coloured and yet, because of all the greens which surround it, this may not be very noticeable. Choose some flower which matches this colour and make a pot-et-fleur and you will see a great difference. Study the plants' colours before you go to shop for the flowers. You will find colours other than greens in stems, stipules, bracts and tendrils.

Use flowers also to accentuate shapes. Irises are attractive when arranged with tall spiky sansevieria possibly because this pot plant's leaves are similar in shape to iris leaves. Arrange pointed gladioli with low

growing large leaves such as begonias. Arrange posies of violets, pansies and tiny cyclamen with little ivies. Use vivid tulips with a vivid cordyline.

Pot-et-fleur can incorporate planted bowls or you can let the plants stay in their pots and arrange them individually. Just the same rules apply as for plant arrangements; you will need suitable containers, a drainage layer and good soil if you are planting the bowl, and plenty of wedging and plunging material if you are arranging plants. If you raise many plants yourself, pot some of these in the black plastic sleeve-type flower pots. As I said elsewhere, you will find these so much more easy to squash into a container than rigid flower pots.

You will need plenty of material for masking and hiding pots and the vessels you use to hold the flowers. The latter can be arranged in many ways. When you fill a bowl you can plant a few empty vessels, deep cream cartons, cigar tubes, small glass or plastic tablet tubes, pointed metal cones which you can buy at the florists' and the plants' roots can find their way round these. You will not then disturb them when you remove the water containers to clean them—flowers die quickly if containers are allowed to become soiled. Keep them as clean as dishes and cutlery. You can also use blocks of foamed plastic inside a small piece of plastic sheeting, this makes it easier to lift out the plastic if you should wish to replace it. After you have made one or two pot-et-fleur arrangements you will soon grasp the essentials.

Of course, many of the plants will hide all the mechanics of the arrangement, but sometimes you will find that a pot rim still shows or the top of a tablet tube appears above plant level. Driftwood, cork bark, coral, sea-fan and sea-shells and dried fungi of many kinds, especially the large bracket-fungi, are some of the accessories you can introduce into pot-et-fleur so that they form part of the design and serve a more useful purpose at the same time.

Do not hesitate either to mix dried materials with your growing plants and fresh flowers. After all, this is nature's way. Dried lotus lily seed heads look extremely lovely used alone or clustered as the focal point surrounded by lively leaves; cocoa palm boats or husks can be arranged with plants other than palms and these will hold flowers, fresh or dried if you wish; so-called dessert-spoons, really the dried ends of agave leaves sometimes sold varnished, will add height and a certain strangeness to familiar plants; skeletonised leaves can be used to back and to throw into contrast those of a more substantial nature.

There really is no limit to the ways you can use flowers and plants to decorate your home.

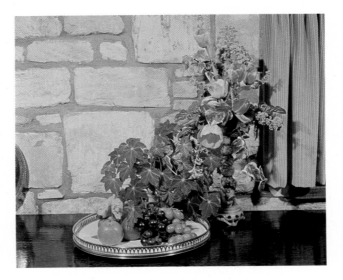

Far left
Regal lilies, dracaena, *Begonia rex*, blue coco beans, camphor pods, cherries and driftwood. Containers with wide tops are best for plant and flower arrangements. There should be space for small flower pots as well as for vessels for the flowers. All can be effectively hidden.

Left
Tulips and scented pelargonium, ivy and garden arum leaves, *Begonia rex* plant and fruit. Plants, flowers and fruit can be grouped together in many ways to make unusual and highly decorative arrangements.

Above
A bowl of growing plants and cut flowers arranged together originally made as a gift. Saintpaulia and crocuses are combined with cut stems of catkins, heather and snowdrops all placed in a kitchen bowl. Other plants could be added quickly and without trouble when the cut flowers have died to make a lasting plant arrangement.

Below left
Wayside grasses, *Hedera canariensis*, and gloxinia. If small flower arrangements and pot plants are concentrated in one area their decorative value is often greater than if they are dispersed. Grasses are long lasting and can be left to dry in situ.

Right
The growing plants framing the carnations are sansevieria, *Hedera helix* 'Glacier' and to the left is the pretty marbled scindapsus and opposite the yellow blotched sedum. Cut sprigs of the silvery senecio to hide pots and flower container.

Harmonising plant and flower colours

In the previous chapter I said that you can often use a few flowers to emphasise some colour in a plant's foliage, and the more you combine and arrange plants and flowers the more you will appreciate the importance of colour harmony.

A simple green plant is likely to suit any setting and if it goes in a green outer pot it will merge discreetly enough with its surroundings. However, you could get much more value from it than that.

Although at first glance they may seem to be so, few leafy plants are in one colour. Even those described as 'green' are unlikely to be produced in one plain definable colour. Such a plant is much more likely to hold many hues of green. It may have tints in its young shoots which are so light and delicate that they seem to offer contrast to the old leaves. Other parts of the same plant may be in deep tones or shades. Often in the oldest leaves there may be a different green on the upperside than there is on the underside. Leaf stipules, tendrils, aerial roots, flowers like those of some of the aeroids, and fruits will extend the variety of hues within this main colour.

Green is a secondary colour of the spectrum, made of a mixture of yellow and blue. In a mixture of plants we can always find some which are more yellow than green and others may have so much blue in them as to be described as glaucous. They all look well together because they are linked by a common colour. Together they make an analogous harmony.

This variation of hue is fascinating and any plant owner will find great enjoyment in discovering just how much variation of one colour exists in one leaf. But there is more to it than that. Many plants, like flowers, have natural colour contrasts and harmonies. Take as a simple example the familiar green rubber plant *Ficus elastica decora*. Often in this plant, perhaps only at certain stages of its growth or times of the year, we can find traces of the most beautiful carmines and magentas. The growing tip may be covered with a vividly coloured sheath. A hue of the same colour, or perhaps a shade, might also be found in the stems or in the raised veins on the underside of the leaf. Many green leaves have beautifully coloured undersides: cinerarias, cyclamen and saintpaulias are familiar examples. Conversely, highly coloured or patterned foliage, begonias for instance, often has plain undersides.

The study of colour is truly fascinating and the purpose of these brief remarks is to suggest that by taking more interest in plant colours we can get greater value from their decorative role in our homes.

Let us refer back to the few simple examples given. It could be that in a furnishing scheme the carmine we see in a rubber plant (incidentally, a natural complementary colour harmony) could give you a lead on what other colours to use in the room where it stands.

Flowering plants in those colours placed near it are likely to have a greater impact and give more pleasure than others. The same applies to flower arrangements, in which, of course, greens can also be blended. Depending on your requirements, containers, some ornaments, pictures, even soft furnishings could follow this guidance.

However, as one can see by the illustrations in this book, plant colour covers the spectrum. Some people have a natural flair for colour, but those who find it difficult to harmonise one colour with another can be helped by the plants and flowers themselves.

If you love plants, then you are bound to admire leaves. As we have already learned, arrangements of different kinds of plants can look very attractive, even when they do not share a flower between them. In a plant arrangement no one colour ever seems to fight or clash with another (although some associations are more exciting than others, as one would expect) and perhaps this is because there is between them the bond of sap—all green brothers under the skin!

The same is true of flowers, but before we deal a little more freely with floral colour harmony I should like to suggest that you experiment with 'flower' arrangements from leaves rather than from cut blooms. A leafy table centre, for instance, is always a good idea. You can keep the arrangement low in stature but very

varied in nature and you can also keep it ever-changing, for it is so easy to take out a faded leaf and slip in some new discovery.

There is no reason why these leaves should be picked from your beloved house plants, although on the other hand there are times when these can be usefully employed. A cyclamen, for instance, which has finished blooming and is beginning to die down is likely to have enough good leaves for you to gather three or four if and when you need them. A rhoicissus, ivy, philodendron, chlorophytum or any plant which is growing just a little too vigorously for your convenience can be pruned from time to time, and there is always the advantage that these prunings can later be treated as cuttings. Indeed, some may even begin to root in water while they are part of the newly created arrangement. This is also often the case with begonia leaves.

Right
The yellow crinkly leaves are cut from stems of forced rhubarb. An arrangement like this uses freshly bought or picked daffodil buds with othe blooms. As these fade, new ones can be bought and the roles reversed.

Far right
Simple complementary colour harmony, orange and blue, but by studying the dahlias and using them as a guide we can elaborate and create a more subtle colour scheme. The ligularia leaves and the interior of the dish repeat the tones in the dahlias' centres.

Below
A combination of preserved beech leaves, pussy willow and dogwood stems with fresh variegated kale, wild ivy trails and cuttings from house plants which include variegated ivies and cordyline leaves.

Other leaves are easy to find, even if you have no garden. Preserved leaves can be used with fresh foliage. Fallen leaves can be pressed and fern fronds treated in ways I have suggested elsewhere. Certain everyday leaves that one does not usually consider as material for flower arrangement can be used, for example, cabbage, parsley, forced rhubarb, beetroot and carrot. Instead of a flower or a flower cluster at the focal point of an arrangement you can use the thick rosettes from any attractive succulent plant.

Some people find great satisfaction in making monochromatic arrangements, in which all kinds of green plant materials play a role. These may include lichened branches, green berries, seed heads, catkins, stems and buds, and as one would expect, green flowers. Actually there are many green flowers, some of them so lowly and inconspicuous that we tend to pass them by unseen. On the other hand, some are so handsome that keen flower arrangers seek them out. Hellebores and spurges are favourites. Grasses also are green flowers. All of these help us to make arrangements full of interest.

Probably one sees more monochromatic arrangements in green than in any other colour because there are so many green plants to be found, but this should not limit you. You can also try to make yellow, blue, brown, orange, carmine or any other colour leaf ensembles. Better still, mix them and see just how vivid and varied you can make a non-flower arrangement.

Once you have experimented with leafy materials alone you may find it helpful to bring in other accessories. Fruits seem a natural addition. Quite often you can arrange these in a temporary decoration, for a dinner party table for instance, and then use the ingredients for a more practical purpose while they are still at their best. However, there are many other fruits than those you buy to eat, hedgerow and garden berries among them, and there are also many attractive vegetables.

As I have already referred to secondary colours, perhaps it would be helpful to give a few more facts, which should help the arranger to create attractive colour harmonies. The colours of flowers and plants are those of the rainbow, in which there are the three primary colours, red, yellow and blue. From these are derived the secondary colours. If you look at a rainbow you will see how naturally these are made. Blue overlaps with yellow to make green; yellow with red to give orange; and if we could bring the two outer edges together as we do when we make an artificial colour wheel, to make its two edges touch, we should see that when the red and blue meet they make purple.

These, then, are the true spectral colours but, as you know, in plant life and elsewhere colours vary considerably. Just think of the number of reds there are, for instance. Some colours are much more definite than we see in the rainbow through strong light. We say that such colours have a rich or strong tone. When colours have a degree of grey or even black in them we call them shades and, as I said earlier, when the colours are thin, i.e. when they contain much light, we say that they are tints. Then there are all the variations which lie between the true colours, the hues, to which we often give descriptive names, such as jade green, turquoise blue, ruby red, primrose yellow, lavender blue and salmon pink.

Each primary spectral colour has its natural opposed secondary colour which is known as its complementary. Thus orange is complementary to blue, green to red and purple to yellow. You can never create a discord if you put two complementaries together. Think how good a green plant looks inside a red pot.

Sometimes the two spectral complementaries are a

123

little too strong for some people's taste when used in flower arrangement. They may prefer to reduce one or both colours to a paler tint. In some settings, for example, a green plant might look better in a pink pot than in a scarlet one. Soft apricot flowers might suit a blue room better than bright orange ones and violet delphiniums be more pleasing against pale lemon walls than against buttercup yellow. Don't imagine though that it is necessary to have equal quantities of complementary colour.

Dealing with flowers and plants differs from handling fabrics and paints because, as we have seen, there is certain to be some other colour or hue present, usually green or some hue of it. So when we are making harmonies we always have to compromise and take this extra colour into account. Actually this can be very useful. Green makes a wonderful buffer between one vivid colour and another. Anyone who is undecided can always select a green container and be almost certain of choosing a harmonious colour for its contents. Of course the green of the vessel could exactly match some green in the plants or flowers and then the harmony would be even more pleasing. It is also safe to take tints to their limit, which of course is white, and shades to theirs, which is black. This means that flowers and plants look right in white or black containers.

There are some other safe colours also. When complementaries are mixed together they make what are known as 'broken' colours. These are pleasing, safe, familiar, almost neutral colours, the natural ones of leaf, bark, branch and stone. Orange and blue make a grey, green and red make a brown, and yellow and purple make a tan. You can often see a natural example of the last in a pansy flower, where you will sometimes see yellow and purple and tan all together. Of course these broken colours will vary according to the quantities of one or other colour in them. Take some water paints and mix them yourself to see what results you get.

So far as flower arrangements are concerned, not everyone likes to see contrasts, even if complementary and therefore harmonious. Many people like to see a more subtle blending of hues. As I have already said, monochromatic arrangements are extremely popular and there is no doubt in my mind that, among these, all-white flower arrangements come highest in popularity, but of course this is a matter of personal taste. Whatever your favourite colour, it really is a fascinating pastime to set about making an arrangement which plays on the colour keyboard from its low shades, through the rich tones and up to the palest tints.

An analogous popular colour harmony is that which uses the neighbouring colours on the spectrum. Thus we can have arrangements in which the flowers go from blue, red to purple; from yellow, orange to red; from yellow, green to blue; but with all the nuances of tints, shades and hues. Many familiar flowers naturally produce blooms in analogous harmony.

If you have to buy all your flowers you might find it difficult to make an arrangement with a wide range of related colours. In this case buy flowers in the two or three colours around which you wish to create the harmony and then use other accessories to increase the colour range and provide the other nuances, the tints, tones and shades.

It goes without saying by now, I hope, that some of these could be leaves, fruits and vegetables. The choice and inclusion of these will have to depend very much on the style and character of the arrangement.

Candles are a great help to the colour-conscious flower arranger and it is well worth while collecting and keeping a stock of these. I suggest that they are used for

Left
Making an arrangement like this is a little like painting a picture, one builds it up slowly introducing light and shade as well as colour. Stems are held in a bowl fitted in the lamp stand. The heavy artichoke was anchored first.

Right
A colour harmony based on some leaf colours. The candles help to bring more of the sap green also found in the variegated kale. The beech is preserved, the maple keys dried. The two flower-like items are the calyces of *Cobea scandens*, an annual climbing plant.

Far right and below
See following page

their colour value alone, but naturally if you wish to light them that is up to you.

If you are making a table setting then you can call in many more aids. Glass and linen as well as candles and fruit can contribute to the colour harmony of the flowers. Even a base on which the arrangement stands can help. Cover or colour it if necessary. Patterned china is often a help in creating colour harmonies, especially simple ones. I have in mind, for example, a few bright orange flowers in a white container which carries matching bands of the flower colour.

As I said earlier, the stem holders such as Oasis make it possible for us to use a plate as a container. If you have one with a patterned or coloured edge, you have a good and useful foundation on which to create a colour scheme. Even if you cannot exactly match the china colour you are almost certain to be able to find either complementary or analogous colours which will set you on your way. Do not overlook the fact that some leaves and other foliage might be more useful from the colour point of view if they are arranged with their undersides uppermost.

Sometimes the colour of the glaze of the interior of a low dish can enhance the floral colour. When flowers are set to one side of such a container and arranged on a pinholder or a block of Oasis, the interior of the vessel is often much more in evidence than the outer surface. This is sometimes worth taking into account when you go to buy or gather your flowers. In the same way, the means you employ to conceal the stem holder can contribute to the colour harmony. Stones, lumps of raw glass, coral and sea shells, can all add one or more hues to the whole.

Do not hesitate, either, to use whole plants as flowers at a focal point in a flower arrangement. You can always slip its pot inside a plastic bag so that it does not get over-watered. Think how attractive a little cyclamen, a variegated cryptanthus or a *Begonia rex* might look under certain circumstances.

Finally, having described so many different combinations and mentioned various combinations encouraging you to mix together plants and flowers, fresh or dried, vegetables, fruits and berries, wood, shells and other accessories, one word of warning: do not forget that it is possible to over-elaborate and that the individual beauty of many plants is often sufficient, depending on their position and type. You can only experiment, and half the joy of plants and flowers is in the fun you can have trying endless variations and combinations to suit your home.

Previous page far right
Christmas colours – red and green – are complementary and we can make a simple yet attractive arrangement by using a handful of evergreens with red accessories. However, the yellow in the holly leaves and the silver down on the senecio prompted the use of silver and gold baubles and honesty.

Previous page below
An arrangement for a summer dining table in which very few blooms are used. Colour comes from the red plastic trug, ornamental kale, aubergines, currant tomatoes, beans, fennel flower, pansies, nasturtiums and three spider chrysanthemums.

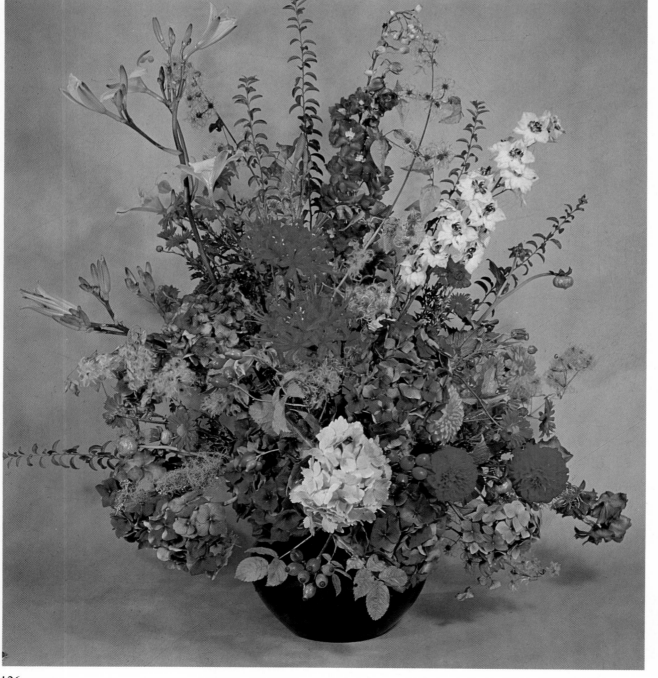

All the spectrum colours are represented here in a rich mixture of autumnal flowers, foliage, berries and seed heads. Few of the flowers are one pure colour. Most have one or more hues which blend them all into one harmonic unit.

126

Index

Acknowledgments

The publishers would like to thank the following individuals and organizations for their kind permission to reproduce the pictures in this book.

A–Z Botanical Collection: 21 above right; 25 above right; 41 above left; 57 above; Agence Top: 6–7; Bernard Alfieri: 14–15 above; 15 below; 18; 47; 50; Julia Clements: 100 centre; Connaissance des Arts (R. Guillemot): 92 above right; W. F. Davidson: 26–27; 51; J. E. Downward: 33 below; 38–39; 40 above; Douglas Fisher Productions: 34; 88–89; A. Huxley: 12 below; 56; 97 above; George Hyde: 16 below; 40–41 below; 41 above right; 43 above;

45 centre; 45 below; Jackson & Perkins: 11; 22 below; Leslie Johns: 1; 4–5; 8–9; 10; 13; 14 below; 20; 21 below; 22 above; 24; 25 left; 27–32; 33 above; 35 above; 35 below; 36; 42; 44 above; 46; 48; 49 above; 49 below; 54; 57 below; 58–87; 90 above; 90 below; 92 above 'eft; 92 below; 94 above; 96; 97 below; 98–99; 100 above; 100 below; 101–103; 105–109; 111–126; Bill McLaughlin: 23; 53; 94 below; 95; NHPA (B. Alfieri): 43 below; W. Schect: 91; Kenneth Scowen: 36–37; 110; Harry Smith Horticultural Photographic Collection: 55; 93; 104; Spectrum Colour Library: 12 above; 15 below right; 16–17 above; 19; 25 below right; W. J. W. Unwin Ltd: 44 below; 45 above.